W9-AFE-703

THE DAY THEY KILLED THE KING

By the same author

History:

THE GUNPOWDER PLOT
KING JAMES I
SIR WALTER RALEIGH
GEORGE VILLIERS, FIRST DUKE OF BUCKINGHAM
JOHN HAMPDEN
CHARLES AND CROMWELL
FOUR STUART PORTRAITS
JEREMY TAYLOR

Essays In Historical Detection:

HISTORICAL WHODUNITS
ENIGMAS OF HISTORY

Historical Plays:

THE CARDINAL'S LEARNING (1530)
HIS EMINENCE OF ENGLAND (1554-1558)
QUEEN ELIZABETH (1581)
GUNPOWDER, TREASON AND PLOT (1605)

Historical Novels:

THE SISTERS (1554-1558)
CAPTAIN THOMAS SCHOFIELD (1648)
THE SILVER BOWL (1660-1662)
JAMES, BY THE GRACE OF GOD (1688)

Historical Places:

CANTERBURY CATHEDRAL
THE ANCIENT CAPITAL (WINCHESTER)

The Execution of King Charles I

THE DAY THEY KILLED THE KING

by

HUGH ROSS WILLIAMSON

New York
THE MACMILLAN COMPANY
1957

First Printing

PRINTED IN THE UNITED STATES OF AMERICA

Library of Congress catalog card number: 57–10708

To

C. V. WEDGWOOD

CONTENTS

ILLUSTRATIONS

PREFACE

THE execution of Charles I is one of the better-known scenes in English history, but it is only fair to warn the reader that almost every detail of it is still hotly debated and that there is conflicting contemporary evidence on many important points.

The moments on the scaffold contain two insoluble historical mysteries—the meaning of the King's famous last word to the Bishop of London: 'Remember' and the identity of the executioners—and of the King's speech on the scaffold, there is more than one version.

Whereas one eyewitness says that he admitted the Prince of Wales's envoy to see the King on the evening of Sunday, January 28, at St. James's, another eyewitness says that he admitted him on Tuesday, January 30, at Whitehall shortly before the execution. One writer gives an account of his meeting and conversation with Fairfax in the corridors of Whitehall just after the King was beheaded, another chronicles that Fairfax was absent from Whitehall all day because he had been put under temporary arrest in his own house in Queen Street. By some, it is said that the King received his last Communion in St. James's before he set out for Whitehall; by others, that Juxon administered it in Whitehall after he had been there for over an hour. The identity of the lady to whom the King sent his ring as a token that she should deliver to the bearer, Thomas Herbert, his casket of jewels is identified by Herbert in one MS. of his *Memoirs* as Jane Whorwood and in another as Lady Wheeler.

No one knows exactly where the scaffold was or which window of the Banqueting House the King stepped through to his death. In spite of a century's controversy on this matter, in which the contending parties have marshalled approximately equal evidence for opposite conclusions, the exact site as well as its shape is unknown. Another topographical mystery is the apartments in which the King waited for death at Whitehall. One of the people who were with him in it calls it 'the Horn-Chamber'; another says it was the Cabinet-Chamber; a third says it was his 'usual bedchamber' which was a considerable distance from the Cabinet-Chamber and in a different part of the Palace.

In trying to make a connected chronicle of the whole day, as far as any evidence is ascertainable—and I can at least claim for this book that it is the first time such a thing has been attempted—I have had to make up my mind not only on these points but on scores of others. But, then, that is the nature of all historical writing. The final conclusion as to 'what really happened' in any historical event depends ultimately on the particular writer's subjective verdict ('subjective,' however carefully 'objective' and 'historically scientific' his method in arriving at it) on the rival credibilities of equally subjective documents. And even when the final reconstruction may seem relatively plausible, there is always the chance that at any moment some new document may come to light which will completely destroy it. For every relevant fact that can be discovered, there are ten thousand which cannot. That is one reason why, in Keyserling's phrase, 'all history is necessarily mythology'; why history can never, by any stretch of definition, be considered a 'science'; and why, as I have been at pains to insist on previous occasions, academic history, when it is not the lowest form of fiction, is only the raw material from which the literary artist may fashion something more nearly corresponding to 'the truth' than is possible for the mere scholastic.

In this book, the most that I can hope is that it will provide a reasonably accurate blue-print for anyone who is interested in what happened in London on a day which, judged by its consequences in retrospect, was one of the most important in the story of Europe and of the world.

HUGH ROSS WILLIAMSON

London, 1956.

FOREWORD

THE execution of King Charles the First on a scaffold in Whitehall on January 30, 1649, is not so very distant if one reckons in lifetimes. I was myself present at, and well remember, the funeral of Florence Nightingale. In the year that she published her famous *Notes on Nursing*, the president of the Social Science Association was Lord Brougham, who has left it on record that his grandmother often told him all the circumstances of the execution of Charles I as she had heard them from an eyewitness in Whitehall.

On the other hand, the events which preceded the unique January day have a different, if equally unfamiliar, perspective. For had there been present at the execution, as there may well have been,[1] one who had enjoyed a span of life equal to that of Florence Nightingale or Lord Brougham's grandmother, he would have been born when Philip of Spain was King of England.

Such a one must have seen the public death of the little Scottish king in simpler terms than any that we, so wise after the event, are capable of understanding. He would have lived through a long period of insecurity, of bitter religious persecution and of two risings against the Crown when Elizabeth was Queen. At the age of thirty he could have taken part in the defeat of the Armada, which finally disappointed Philip's hopes of again occupying the English throne. He would have seen a change of dynasty, in which James of Scotland, as one of a dozen or so claimants with approximately equal rights, had been put on the English

[1] Charles I, for example, talked to 'Old Parr', who was well over a hundred and told the King details of the dissolution of the Monasteries.

throne. He would have found the new King's entourage of foreign Scots who plundered places hardly less obnoxious and certainly not less 'foreign' than Philip's Spanish courtiers. He would have seen a bankrupt England fall so low in Europe that West Country fishermen dared not put to sea for fear of the Barbary pirates who landed with impunity on English soil, burnt English towns and carried off English men, women and children as slaves. He would have known the day when, to public rejoicing, an all-powerful favourite, dictator in everything but name, was assassinated in a Portsmouth inn—an event to be followed by the execution of another 'first minister' and of an Archbishop of Canterbury. He would have experienced the long years of social and political unrest which culminated in two civil wars. And the last act, the death of the King who had brought about those two wars and could not be trusted not to precipitate a third, might well have seemed to him a practical necessity of no great moment.

Certainly the action would lack the constitutional overtones which, seen in retrospect, make it without parallel in English history. Kings had indeed been defeated in battle by their countrymen to be officially deposed and unofficially murdered by the victors; but at least those victors claimed the vacant throne by some sort of right. They were merely the 'pares' changing their 'primus' by the conventional—and, indeed, the only possible—method. But a king defeated by a popular army and subsequently tried and executed by his subjects as a public act of witness to novel constitutional theories was a singular phenomenon, for which there were no precedents. Though Cromwell, a Conservative empiricist, tried to impose a veneer of legality on the action, it is difficult to suppose that so stern a realist succeeded in deceiving himself or that his own contempt for the tribunal he had been forced to create was any less than Charles's. With one voice, the entire legal profession of England, even those noted for their extreme anti-Royalism, had refused to have anything to do with what they denounced as a judicial farce. Young Algernon Sidney put the matter in a nutshell when he told Cromwell bluntly: "First, the King can be tried by no court; second, no man can be tried by this court." No English lawyer could be found to draw up the charge, which was eventually entrusted to an accommodating alien. The House of Lords, however intimidated, refused to pass the necessary Ordinance. Even when what was left of the House of Commons appointed 135 'safe' judges, fifty of them declined to sit.

It is, indeed, to misconceive the trial and execution of Charles I even to think in terms of constitutional correctness. The legal mind here introduces that same touch of fantasy as surrounds the long academic argument which preceded the trial of the Regicides eleven years later: should the killing of the King on January 30, 1649, be alleged as having taken place on the last day of King Charles I or on the first day of King Charles II? As the law does not recognize any fraction of a day, the whole day must be in one reign or the other. The judges were quite unable to come to a conclusion on this vital point, some thinking that the same day might be entirely within both reigns and others doubting it. Eventually they solved the difficulty by charging the prisoners, not with killing the King on January 30, but with compassing his death on January 29, which was undoubtedly in the reign of Charles I.

But the trial and execution of the Regicides, though so eminently 'constitutional,' was as simply an act of political vengeance as the 'unconstitutional' trial and execution of the King was an act of political necessity. And perhaps Quin, the actor, made the best comment on pedantic pretence when, in reply to Bishop Warburton's challenge: "By what law do you justify Charles's execution?" he retorted: "By all the laws he had left them."

The true constitutional issue which dominated the proceedings was of a very different nature. It concerned the basis of government. Ever since the Army had become the master of the country, the one question interminably debated was whether a complete break should be made with the traditional Constitution and England try the experiment of government by a single House of Parliament elected biennially by manhood suffrage without any property qualification. The document in which this was embodied was known as *The Agreement of the People*, which was to the seventeenth century all that the *Social Contract* was to the eighteenth and the *Communist Manifesto* to the late nineteenth and twentieth. Had the *Agreement* been put into effect, it would have meant that England made in 1649 a constitutional 'levelling' experiment which she has not made fully yet and did not even begin to make till 1884.

The popular protagonist of the *Agreement* was the Leveller, Colonel Thomas Rainsborough: its Conservative opponent was Oliver Cromwell. From the May of 1647 to the November of 1648, their names were of equal and outstanding importance. When, in the autumn of 1647, Rainsborough flung at Cromwell 'One of us must not live,' it was—as the French agent in London duly reported—a matter of speculation in Westminster whether Cromwell would survive. But it was Rainsborough who was murdered and it was his assassination on October 29, 1648, which made inevitable Charles's execution three months later.

In the autumn of 1647, Cromwell was working for the restoration of Charles to the throne, with himself as his 'first minister.' "The King personally, the monarchy politically, were as safe in the summer of 1647 as Queen Victoria and her monarchy in the summer of 1847," as Mr. G. M. Young has expressed it. Yet, a year later, Cromwell forced the King's execution.

As long as Rainsborough was alive, leading the 'Left',

Cromwell in the 'Centre' could incline, with Fairfax on the extreme 'Right,' to constitutional Royalism as preferable to Communism. But once Rainsborough was dead, he had no alternative to adopting his murdered rival's policy in so far as it involved the destruction of the monarchy. He had to dispose of the King before he could turn and dispose of the Levellers.

Cromwell's desertion of the King was made easier by two other circumstances, one personal, one politico-religious, but both springing from Charles's chronic duplicity. During the period of the 'Hampton Court negotiations,' Cromwell was sleeping in a different place each night to avoid assassination by the Levellers, who accused him of betraying the people's cause by even seeing the King. But this risk, and much more, Cromwell was prepared to run if he and Charles could arrive at a solution which should ensure an efficient and stable government. Unfortunately for the King, Cromwell intercepted one of his letters to the Queen in France in which he explained that he had no intention of 'yielding to the traitor' whom he meant to hang in due time and that 'she need not have any concern in her mind, for whatever agreement they might enter into, he should not look upon himself obliged to keep any promises made so much on compulsion whenever he had power enough to break them.'[1] This was fair enough. Cromwell may, indeed, be convicted of over-ingenuousness in not having postulated it. But, in the event, he disliked being made so patently a fool.

The King's other exploit had more serious repercussions. Having fled from Hampton Court because he was afraid that the Levellers intended to murder him, he took refuge in the Isle of Wight. Though a prisoner, he was given permission to see Scottish Commissioners, ostensibly to discuss the

[1] I have given my reasons for supposing the 'Saddle Letter' genuine in my *Charles and Cromwell*, p. 183 n.

general constitutional situation, really to sign the 'Engagement' by which, in return for a Scottish invasion of England, he promised, when restored to power, to establish Presbyterianism as the State religion of England and to take all possible measures 'for suppressing the opinions and practices of Independents and all such doctrines and practices as are contrary to the light of nature or to the known principles of Christianity.' He also promised to admit to the English Privy Council "a considerable and competent number of Scotsmen" and a third part of the persons employed in places of trust about the Royal family were always to be Scots.

This precipitated the Second Civil War, for which Charles alone was undoubtedly responsible, whatever view may be taken of the reasons for the First. It made him in the eyes of Cromwell and the Army the 'Man of Blood,' who must expiate the slaughter with his own life. But it also emphasised two aspects of the King's personality which posterity is apt to forget—his fundamental Scottishness and his attitude to Anglicanism which, though he safeguarded it for himself and his entourage, he was prepared to sacrifice in the country. The 'Blessed Martyr' theory has never taken sufficient account of the fact that, in the last analysis, Charles was put to death because he undertook to establish Presbyterianism at the point of Scottish swords as the State religion of England.

And his attitude was no new thing or a sudden reversal of policy by a man in a desperate situation. The seeds of it had been sown in his childhood. In the first place he was a Scot—the only English blood in him came, thinly, from a great-great-grandmother—brought up by Scots, speaking to the end of his life with a Scots accent, and looking always on the Scots as his friends and compatriots. "He was always an immoderate lover of the Scottish nation," Clarendon complained, "having not only been born there, but educated by that people and besieged by them always, having few English about him till he was king, and the major number of his servants being still of those who, he thought, could never fail him."

From his earliest days, Charles grew to understand Presbyterianism so well that, when he was seventeen and his father was taken so ill that it seemed likely that he would then succeed to the throne, Lancelot Andrewes, Bishop of Ely, bewailed 'the sad condition of the Church if God should at that time determine the days of the King; the Prince then being conversant only with Scotchmen which made up the greatest part of his family and were ill-affected to the worship of the Church of England.'

In later years, when, under the influence of Laud, the chaplain of his beloved Buckingham, he became the champion of the Church of England, this early training was not eradicated. Always he was able to regard Presbyterianism as a religious (though not as a political) alternative for his people, if not for himself.

Cromwell, on the other hand, who was brought up in the Church of England became, like Fairfax and Rainsborough, an Independent (or, as they would be called to-day, Congregationalist) and disliked the presbyter only slightly less than the priest. He respected, even if he disagreed with Charles's Anglicanism; but he could not forgive Charles's tenderness to Presbyterianism. And this exasperation was increased by the difference in nationality. To Cromwell, fiercely, even parochially, English, the Scots were foreigners. Charles's final action in calling in the Scottish army was, he wrote, "a more prodigious Treason than any that had been perpetrated before" because its intention was "to vassalize us to a *foreign* nation."

Thus at the end of November 1648, as far as can be ascertained, Cromwell, unchallenged leader (though not titular head) of a victorious and predominantly republican army, decided to kill the King as a 'cruel necessity.' From Charles the spectre of death had never been far since he had become a prisoner of his enemies, though, familiar with the stories of defeated kings, he had envisaged assassination; and when a fanatical Leveller, Colonel Thomas Harrison, was sent to escort him to Windsor, he immediately suspected that the instrument of his end had been appointed.

Nothing could have been further from the truth or have more vividly illustrated Charles's misconception of the men and ideas he was fighting. When Harrison himself came to trial as a regicide, he was proud to proclaim: "The matter was not a thing done in a corner. I believe the sound of it hath been in most nations." It was in the very spirit of Brutus's attitude to Caesar:

> Let's kill him boldly, but not wrathfully;
> Let's carve him as a dish fit for the gods,
> Not hew him as a carcass fit for hounds

that Cromwell and his associates brought their anointed King to public trial and death.

PROLOGUE TO THE DAY

(i) The Trial

Charles refuses to plead

ABOUT two o'clock in the afternoon of Saturday, January 20, 1649, King Charles I faced his judges in Westminster Hall, which, with the King's Standard that had been captured at Naseby hanging from the great roof, was set for a trial. The last time it had served this purpose was when Strafford was impeached. The booths of the tradesmen which usually ranged along the walls had been removed. The entrance to the Taverns (named Hell, Purgatory and Paradise) much frequented by lawyers' clerks, was bricked up. Against the west window, rising nearly to the centre of it, tiers of benches had been erected for the Commissioners. Each side of them, running along the north and south walls, were temporary galleries for ladies and other privileged spectators. On a dais in the centre of the tribunal was a crimson velvet chair with a judge's desk before it for Bradshawe, the Lord President of the Court—a little-known lawyer from the North who had become popular by describing the King as 'Nero.'

Facing his chair at some little distance, was another crimson velvet chair for the prisoner.

Behind this, and about forty feet from the Commissioners' benches, a serviceable railing crossed the Hall and all the space below it was at the disposal of any citizens of London who cared to attend or who could manage to gain entry to the trial of their King.

The scene was a blaze of scarlet. The benches and seats for the Commissioners were draped with scarlet cloth. The soldiers who lined the Hall, guarded the windows, kept open the passages, intimidated the crowd, stood in a hollow square round the King, were in the red coats of the Guards. The officers, under Colonel Daniel Axtell, who was in charge of the Hall, were in full-dress scarlet uniform, carrying their gold-headed canes.

Isolated, Charles sat in this sea of red, his tall black hat on his head and his dark suit throwing into still greater prominence the vivid blue of the broad Garter ribbon round his neck, and accentuating the pallor of the white, stern face.

On the face that day, there was a new look.[1] There was strength and purpose as never before. The tired, sad eyes were alive and accusing and not a little contemptuous. It may be that he was at ease, with a certainty of himself and his cause, as he had never in his life been at ease before. Certainly then, for the only time in his life, his stammer left him. And with the impediment in his speech had gone also the duplicity of his mind—and the need for it. Step by step, he had been forced back to the essentials which, whatever the price or the plausibility, he could not betray. He was dying, quite simply, for the rights of his order, the constitution of his country and the authority of his Church. And now in this farce which preceded death, he had one only duty—so to bear himself that, when the day of revolution, military despotism and heresy was over, posterity should know that he had kept faith.

When he came into the Hall he had been met by the serjeant-at-arms with the mace and escorted by him to the chair at the bar. He sat down quietly, without removing his hat, but almost immediately rose and scanned the faces of those present in search of some he knew. Of the sixty-seven Commissioners facing him, he could recognize only eight. On the third tier, sitting under the Arms of England and

[1] There is a portrait of him in Westminster Hall by Bower, now in All Souls College, Oxford.

Ireland, which had been substituted for the Royal Arms, he saw Oliver Cromwell.

Cromwell and his son-in-law Ireton alone of the general officers were present. Not only had Fairfax declined ("Not here and never will be; he has too much sense," shouted Lady Fairfax from the spectators' gallery when his name was called), but all Cromwell's equals—Desborough and Fleetwood, Skippon and Lambert and Haselrig—were absent. There were present only the hard core of "Cromwellian Colonels", those who were frankly his "creatures" like Downes (and there was to be trouble even with him) and those who owed social advancement to his perception of their military efficiency—Okey, the ship-chandler, and Pride, the brewer's drayman; Ewer, the serving-man, and Horton, Haselrig's servant; the cobbler Hewson and the salter Goffe. Thomas Harrison and other Levellers were there: three London aldermen; some deserters from Charles—the renegade courtier Mildmay and the bankrupt Danvers and the half-lunatic Monson; and a sprinkling of men of no account, like the weak and shifty Millington, who were later to plead that they had been forced into service by Cromwell.

It was, indeed, Cromwell's affair. As he had created out of the poor material at his disposal a mighty instrument to take and rule the kingdom, so now, in another medium, he moulded another tool to kill the King. But his making of the Army had been dictated to him by events; it had been undeliberate, a concession to necessity. The High Court was an expression of his individual will and purpose. And he was not at ease. His energy, indeed, was demonic; but it was not the old, quiet power. His state of hysterical exaltation seemed not far removed from madness.

On the day when Charles had been brought from Windsor to be lodged in Sir Robert Cotton's house near Westminster Hall, Cromwell at a window had caught sight of the King as he landed. He had turned "white as a wall" and asked the others in the room: "My masters, he is come, he is come, and now we are doing that great work that the whole nation will be full of. Therefore I desire you to let us resolve here what answer we shall give the King when he comes before us, for the first question he will ask us will be by what authority and commission do we try him?" After a silence, someone had suggested: "In the name of the Commons and Parliament assembled and all the good people of England." It sounded well; but none knew better than Cromwell that it was as impossible in law as it was equivocal in statement.

*BRADSHAWE: Charles Stuart, King of England, the Commons of England assembled in Parliament, being sensible of the evils and calamities that have been brought upon this nation and of the innocent blood that hath been shed in it, which is fixed upon you as the principal author of it, have resolved to make inquisition for this blood, and according to that fundamental power that is vested, and trust reposed in them by the people (other means failing through your default) have resolved to bring you to trial and judgment, and have therefore constituted this High Court of justice, before which you are now brought; where you are to hear your charge, upon which the Court will proceed according to justice.

CHARLES: By your favour, hold!

BRADSHAWE: The Court commands the charge shall be read; if you have anything to say after, the Court will hear you. Clerk, read the charge.

CLERK: A charge of High Treason and other high crimes exhibited to the High Court of Justice by John Cook,

* In the following abstract of the trial, the speeches have necessarily been selected and shortened but the balance and the arguments have, I hope, remained undistorted.

Where the connecting passages are in quotation marks, they are from contemporary accounts. Where they are without them, they are my own abstracts.

Esq., Solicitor General appointed by the said Court, for and on behalf of the People of England against Charles Stuart, King of England:

That he the said Charles Stuart being admitted King of England and therein trusted with a limited power to govern by and according to the laws of the land and not otherwise, and by his trust oath and office being obliged to use the power committed to him for the good and benefit of the people and the preservation of their rights and liberties; yet, nevertheless, out of a wicked design to erect and uphold in himself an unlimited and tyrannical power, to rule according to his will and to overthrow the rights and liberties of the people, he, the said Charles Stuart, for the accomplishment of such his design and for the protecting of himself and his adherents, in his own and their wicked practices to the same ends, hath traitorously and maliciously levied war against the present Parliament and the people therein represented. Particularly on or about the thirtieth day of June, in the year of our Lord 1642 at Beverley . . .

"The prisoner, whilst the charge was reading, sat down again in his chair, looking sometimes at the High Court and sometimes up to the galleries. And having risen again and turned about to behold the guards and spectators, sat down again, looking very sternly and with a countenance not at all moved, till these words: 'Charles Stuart, to be a tyrant, traitor,' etc., were read, at which he laughed as he sat, in the face of the Court."

CLERK: . . . doth for the said treasons and crimes, on behalf of the said people of England impeach the said Charles Stuart as a tyrant, traitor, murderer and implacable enemy to the commonwealth of England.

(*Charles laughs.*)

BRADSHAWE: Sir, you have now heard your charge read. The Court expect your answer and are willing to hear it.

CHARLES: First I must know by what power I am called hither before I will give answer. I was not long ago in the Isle of Wight. How I came there is a longer story than I think fit at this time to speak of, but there I entered into a treaty with the two Houses of Parliament, with as much public faith as is possible to be had with any people in the world. I treated there with a number of Lords and gentlemen and treated honestly and uprightly. I cannot say but they dealt very nobly with me; we were upon a conclusion of the treaty. Now I would know by what authority (I mean lawful, for there are many unlawful authorities in the world, robbers by the highway, taking men's purses by illegal ways)—but I would know by what authority—lawful—I was carried thence and was since brought from place to place like I know not what, till I came hither. That I would fain know. When I know a lawful authority, then I will answer.

Remember, I am your King, your lawful King and what sin you bring upon your heads; besides those other judgments you bring upon the land. Think well upon it, I say; think well upon it, before you go from one sin to a greater. I know no authority you have. Therefore let me know by what lawful authority I am seated here and I shall not be unwilling to answer. In the meantime, know I will not betray my trust. I have a trust committed to me by God, by old and lawful descent. I will not betray that trust to answer to a new unlawful authority, for all the world. Therefore, let me know by what lawful authority I am come hither and you shall hear more of me.

BRADSHAWE: Sir, if you had been pleased to observe what was intimated to you in the paper read, you would have known by what authority you came hither—by the authority of the Commons of England, assembled in Parliament, on behalf of the People of England, by which people you are elected King.

CHARLES: I deny that. England was never an elective kingdom. It has been an hereditary kingdom for near a thousand years. Your authority, raised by a usurped power, I will never—I will never betray my trust. I am entrusted with the liberty of my people. I do stand more for the liberties of my people than anyone that is seated here as a judge. Therefore show me by what lawful authority I am seated here and I will answer it. Otherwise I will not betray the liberties of my people.

BRADSHAWE: Whether you have not betrayed your trust will appear in good time when you have given your answer. You, instead of answering, interrogate the Court, which doth not become you in this condition.

CHARLES: I do not come here as submitting to the Court. Let me see a legal authority, warranted either by the Word of God, by Scripture, or warranted by the ancient laws and constitutions of the realm and I will answer.

BRADSHAWE: Sir, you have propounded a question and received an answer. Sir, the interpretation doth not belong to you. If you acknowledge not the authority of the Court, the Court must proceed and consider what to do with you. In the meantime those that brought you hither will take charge of you again. And, sir, you will do well to consider whether this be all the answer you insist on.

CHARLES: Sir, I desire that you will give me and all the world satisfaction in this, for let me tell you, it is not a present power that will settle the business of this kingdom. I have sworn to maintain the peace by the duty I owe to God and my country and I will do it to the last breath of my body. Therefore, sir, you shall do well to satisfy first God and then the country by what lawful authority you do it. If you do it by a usurped authority, it will not last long and there is a God in Heaven that will call you—and those that gave you authority—to account for it. Therefore, satisfy me in that and then I will answer you. Otherwise I betray my trust. For I do avow that it is as great a sin to withstand lawful authority as to submit to a tyrannical, or any other way unlawful, authority. Therefore, satisfy God and me and all the world in that, and you shall receive my answer. I am not afraid of this business.

SPECTATORS: God save Your Majesty!

BRADSHAWE: The Court expects that you should give them a positive answer. Their purpose is to adjourn till Monday next. If you then persist in the same temper you are in now, this is as much as if you had said nothing to us. We are upon God's and the kingdom's errand, and that peace we stand for will be better had and kept when justice is done. We are satisfied. Therefore consider what you have to do at your next appearance.

CHARLES: If you will show me what lawful authority you have I shall be satisfied. To *say* you have lawful authority will satisfy no reasonable man.

BRADSHAWE: We who are your judges think it reasonable. The Court has heard you and you are to be disposed of as they have commanded. The guard are accordingly commanded to withdraw the prisoner.

CHARLES: The King!

CRIER: Oyez! Oyez! Oyez! This Court doth adjourn itself till Monday morning next at nine of the clock.

"His Majesty being returned to Cotton House, where by Sir Thomas Cotton, the master of the House and Mr. Kinnersley of the wardrobe, the King's chamber had the best accommodation that could so suddenly be made. The soldiers that were upon the guard were in the next chamber to the King's. His Majesty commanded Mr. Herbert to bring a pallet; and, being laid on the matted floor, at one side of the King's bed, there slept.

"Sunday, the 21st January, Dr. Juxon that good Bishop of London had (as His Majesty desired) the liberty to attend the King, which was much to his comfort, and (as he said) no small refreshing to his spirit in that his uncomfortable condition. The most part of the day was spent in prayer and preaching to the King.

"Monday, the 22nd of January, Col. Hacker brought His Majesty the second time before the Court, then sitting as formerly, in Westminster Hall. So soon as His Majesty came into the Hall some soldiers made a hideous cry for Justice! Justice! some of the officers joining with them. At which uncouth noise the King seemed somewhat abashed, but overcame it with patience."

BRADSHAWE: Sir, you will remember at the last Court you were pleased to make some scruple that you knew not by what authority you were brought hither. The Court hath since that time taken into their serious consideration what you then said and they are satisfied fully with their authority and they hold it fit you should stand satisfied therewith too. Their authority they avow to the whole world; the whole kingdom is to rest satisfied with it; and you are to rest satisfied with it. Sir, the Court expects you to apply yourself to the charge, not to lose any more time, but to give a positive answer thereto.

CHARLES: If it were only my own particular case, I would have been satisfied with the protestation I made last time I was here against the legality of this Court and that a King cannot be tried by any superior jurisdiction on earth. But it is not my case alone. It is the freedom and liberty of the people of England. And—whatever you may pretend—I must justly stand for their liberties. For if power without law may make law, may alter the fundamental laws of the kingdom, then I do not know what subject in England can be assured of his life or anything he can call his own. Therefore, when I came here, I expected particular reasons to know by what law, what authority you proceed against me. And since I cannot persuade you to do it, I shall tell you my reasons as short as I can.

These are my reasons why in conscience of that duty I owe to God first and my people afterwards for their lives, liberties and estates I conceive I cannot answer until I be satisfied with the legality of the Court. First: All proceedings against any man whatsoever——

BRADSHAWE: Sir, I must interrupt you, which I would not willingly do but that what you do is not agreeable to any Court of justice, as all who know what belongs to justice know. Sir, it seems you are about to enter into arguments and disputes about the authority of this Court before which you are brought as a prisoner and charged as an high delinquent. You may not do it. You are to give your direct answer, either affirmative or negative, whether you will answer your charge or not; and what your answer is.

CHARLES: Sir, by your favour, I do not know the forms of law; but I do know law and reason. Though I am no lawyer professed, I know as much law as any gentleman of England; and therefore, sir, (by your favour) I do plead for the liberties of the people more than any of you do. And therefore if I should impose a belief upon any man without reasons given for it, it were unreasonable. I must tell you that by that reason that I have, as thus informed, I cannot yield unto it——

BRADSHAWE: I must again interrupt you; you may not go on in that course. You speak of law and reason. It is fit there should be law and reason—and both are against you in

The Banqueting Hall and surrounding buildings as they were in 1649

Hugh Peters

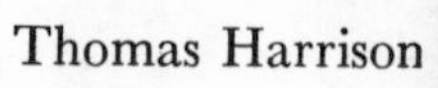

Thomas Harrison

the proceedings. The vote of the Commons of England in Parliament—that is the reason of the kingdom. It is the law of the kingdom; and these are they that have given you that law according to which you should have ruled and reigned. Sir, you are not to dispute our authority: you are told it again by the Court. Sir, it will be taken notice of that you stand in contempt of the Court. Your disputes are not to be admitted and your contempt will be recorded.

CHARLES: I do not know how a King can be a delinquent; but, by all the law I ever heard of, all men, delinquents or what you will, may put in a demurrer. To demur against any proceedings is legal. I do demand that and demand to be heard with my reasons.

BRADSHAWE: The Court over-rules your demurrer. You are called here to account by the authority of the Court. We sit here by the authority of the Commons of England and that authority hath called your ancestors—the greatest of them—to account.

CHARLES: I deny that. Show me one precedent.

BRADSHAWE: Sir, you ought not to interrupt while the Court is speaking to you. This point is not to be debated by you; neither will the Court permit you to do it.

CHARLES: I say, sir, by your favour, that the Commons of England was never a Court of judicature. I would know how they came to be so.

BRADSHAWE: You are not permitted to go on with these discourses. Clerk of the Court!

CLERK: Charles Stuart, King of England, you have been accused by the people of England of high treason and other high crimes and treasons; which hath been read unto you. The Court, having determined that you ought to answer the same, require you to give a positive answer, whether you confess or deny the charges.

CHARLES: I will answer the same so soon as I know by what authority you sit.

BRADSHAWE: If this is all that you will say, then (*speaking to the guards*) gentlemen, you that brought the prisoner hither conduct him back again.

CHARLES: I do desire to give in my reasons. I shall not speak anything without reason. I do require that I may give in my reasons why I do not——

BRADSHAWE: Sir, 'tis not for prisoners to require.

CHARLES: Sir, I am not an ordinary prisoner.

BRADSHAWE: Serjeant-at-arms, take away the prisoner.

CHARLES: You have not heard my reasons yet.

BRADSHAWE: Your reasons are not to be heard against the highest jurisdiction.

CHARLES: Show me that highest jurisdiction where reason is not to be heard. Show me wherever the House of Commons was a Court of judicature.

BRADSHAWE: Serjeant, take away the prisoner.

CHARLES: Well, sir, remember that the King is not at liberty to give in his reasons for the liberty and freedom of his subjects.

(*Here there is a great shout from the people of 'God save the King', which is quelled by the guards.*)

BRADSHAWE: Sir, you are not to have liberty to use such language. How great a friend you have been to the laws and liberties of the people, let all England and the world judge.

CHARLES: Under favour, sir, it was the liberty, freedom and laws of the subject, that I took—defended myself with arms. I never took arms against the people, but for the laws.

HEWSON: Justice! Justice! Upon the traitor!

(*He spits in Charles's face.*)

CHARLES: Well, sir! God hath justice in store both for you and me.

"As His Majesty returned from the Hall to Cotton House, a soldier that was upon the guard said aloud as the King passed by, 'God bless you, sir.' The King thanked him; but an uncivil officer struck him with his cane upon the head; which His Majesty observing said: The punishment exceeded the offence. Being come to his apartment in Cotton House, he immediately, upon his knees, went to prayer. Afterwards he asked Mr. Herbert if he had heard that cry of the soldiers for justice? Who answered, he did, and marvelled thereat. 'So did I not,' said the King, 'for I am well assured the soldiers bear no malice to me; the cry was, no doubt, given by their officers, for whom the soldiers would do the like, were there occasion.' Tuesday, the 23rd of January, the King was the third time summoned and, as formerly, guarded to the Court; where as at other times, he persisted in his judgment that they had no legal jurisdiction or authority to proceed after that manner against him."

BRADSHAWE: Sir, I must let you know from the Court, as their commands, that you are not to be permitted to issue out into any other discourses till such time as you have given a positive answer to the charge that is now against you; and this is their final command.

CHARLES: For the charge, I value it not a rush. It is the liberties of the people of England that I stand for. For me to acknowledge a new Court that I never heard of before—I, that am your King, that should be an example to all the people of England to uphold justice, to maintain the old law—indeed I know not how to do it. You spoke very well the first day that I came here, of the obligation that I had laid upon me by God for the maintenance of the liberties of my people to defend (as much as in me lies) the ancient laws of the kingdom. That obligation, *you* spoke of. And therefore until I am shown that this is not against the fundamental laws of the kingdom, by your favour, sir, I can put in no particular answer. If you will give me time, I will show my reason why I cannot do it——

BRADSHAWE: Clerk, do your duty.

CHARLES: Duty!

CLERK: Charles Stuart, King of England, you are accused in behalf of the People of England of divers high crimes and treasons; which charge hath been read to you. The Court now requires you to give your final and positive answer by way of confession or denial of the charge.

CHARLES: Sir, I say again to you, if I might give satisfaction to the People of England that I have done nothing against that trust that hath been committed to me, I will do it. But to acknowledge a new Court against their privileges, sir, you must excuse me.

BRADSHAWE: Sir, this is the third time that you have publicly disowned this Court and put an affront upon it. How far you have preserved the freedom of the subject, your actions have spoken it. You have written your meaning in bloody characters throughout the whole kingdom. The Court understands your meaning. Clerk, record the default. And gentlemen, you that brought the prisoner, take him back again.

CHARLES: I have one word to you. If it were only my own particular case, indeed I would not——

BRADSHAWE: Sir, you have heard the pleasure of the Court and you will find, though you will not admit it, that you are before a Court of justice.

CHARLES: I find I am before a power.

(*Shouts of 'God save the King' and 'God save the Kingdom of England.'*)

Cromwell and Fairfax

That Tuesday evening, the King's enemies found that affairs had reached a crisis. The King's stubbornness in his refusal to plead was defeating them. With each appearance, his cause had gained in strength. From every quarter appeals and threats were pouring in in an attempt to save his life. Even the Presbyterian clergy were preaching in his favour. The Scots Commissioners sent in their third protest. The attendance of the judges was still scanty and even among those who sat there were signs of wavering. There were even rumours that Fairfax, as Lord General of the Army, might use his authority to rescue the King. The one way in which the balance might be redressed was if Fairfax could be induced to take his place with the judges at the next sitting.

Fairfax refused to leave his house in Queen Street, but his wife, who was present in one of the galleries at the trial, was able to report all the proceedings to him.

FAIRFAX: How does the King bear himself?

LADY FAIRFAX: Like a king. He is very majestic and bears himself resolutely, though they say he has not slept these two nights. He was troubled only once when he was leaning on his staff and the gold head broke off suddenly. They are saying someone tampered with it. But however that came about, the stranger thing is that the King speaks freely and without the stammer that has always troubled him. I tell you he shames the traitors who are pretending to judge him.

That night Cromwell came to Fairfax's house to try to persuade him to take his place in Westminster Hall. Though no record exists of the interview, Cromwell's arguments for the legality of the trial are known.

CROMWELL: A breach of trust in a king ought to be punished more than any crime whatsoever. What, are all those on whom public justice has been done—his creatures and servants, small offenders acting by commission from the King—to suffer and he, who is the principal and so the most guilty to escape? And, if we let him go, shall not we be punished for it at the judgment of God? We know in him a disposition so bent to the ruin of all the righteous and just things we have contended for, that it is on my conscience that, if we do not execute justice upon him, God will require at our hands all the blood and desolation that will ensue, if we suffer him to escape now that God has brought him into our hands. In bringing in the Scots, did he not commit a more prodigious treason than any that had been perpetrated before; because the former quarrel was that Englishmen might rule over one another; this to vassalize us to a foreign nation.

To the argument which young Algernon Sidney used and which, probably, Fairfax also used—first, the King can be tried by no Court; second, this Court can try no man—Cromwell and his associates would answer:

CROMWELL: The end of having kings, or any other governors, it is for the enjoying of justice; that is the end. The King must understand that he is but an officer in trust and he ought to discharge that trust. If he betrays that trust—as all England and all the world that has looked upon it hath seen that he hath done—where should the remedy lie but in Parliament. Parliaments were ordained to that purpose—to redress the grievances of the people. The King has a master; the law is his master; and the law is the Acts of Parliament. We must act in this as having always God before our eyes—that God whom we know is King of Kings and Lord of Lords; that God with whom

> there is no respect of persons; that God who is the avenger of innocent blood; we have that God before us; that God who doth bestow a curse upon them that withhold their hands from shedding of blood in the case of guilty malefactors who do deserve death. That God we have before our eyes and were it not so, then our Court *were* but an appearance. But it is so—that it is so is writ large by many marvellous signs these seven years, by his crimes which all the land may witness—and we must do our duty without any respect to any but God and what is laid upon us by his Justice. It is great work we are doing.

"The Lord General was baited with fresh dogs all Tuesday night to bring him into the Hall on the morrow to countenance the business; but by no means would he consent."

Protests

No one went into the Hall next day. In an attempt to gain time to strengthen the waverers, as well as to prevent a further public appearance of the King, the intended sitting was abandoned and the Court met in private to hear additional evidence "for the further satisfaction of themselves." They did so again on Thursday, by which time the number of Commissioners had shrunk to thirty-one. On Friday, still in private, they decided to resume the public sitting next day, not to try but to sentence the King. Cromwell and some others signed the death-warrant in advance. They knew, from spies, that the King intended to appeal from the Court to the two Houses of Parliament; from the admittedly illegal body to one which, since it would be King, Lords and Commons assembled, was in fact the constitutional law-making power of the realm. Bradshawe was given careful instructions as to how to circumvent this move on the King's part, and when he rose in his place on the morning of Saturday, January 27, he spoke not to the King, who was sitting in front of him, but to the people.

BRADSHAWE: Gentlemen——

CHARLES: I shall desire a word to be heard a little; and I hope I shall give no occasion of interruption.

BRADSHAWE: You may answer in your time. Hear the Court first.

CHARLES: If it please you, sir, I desire to be heard. It will be in order to what I believe the Court will say—a hasty judgment is not so soon recalled.

BRADSHAWE: Sir, you shall be heard before the judgment is given; and in the meantime you may forbear.

CHARLES: I *shall* be heard before the judgment be given?

BRADSHAWE: You shall. (To the people) Gentlemen, it is well known to most or all of you here present that the prisoner at the bar hath been several times brought before the Court to make answer to a charge of high treason and other high crimes exhibited against him in the name of the People of England——

LADY FAIRFAX: Not half or a quarter of them. Oliver Cromwell is a traitor.

AXTELL: Present your muskets and shoot them if they say another word.

SPECTATOR: It's Lady Fairfax. There's no doubt it's Lady Fairfax.

BRADSHAWE: Order! Order!

AXTELL: What drab is this who dares disturb the Court? Fetch her down.

SPECTATOR: She's gone. . . .

BRADSHAWE: As the prisoner has proved contumacious and refused to submit to answer the Court, they have thought fit to take the whole matter into their consideration. And they are resolved and are agreed upon a sentence to be pronounced against this prisoner. But as he doth desire to be heard before sentence is pronounced, the Court will hear him. (*To Charles*) Sir, if that which you have to say be to offer any debate concerning the jurisdiction of this Court, as you have formerly done, you will not be heard. But if you have anything to say in defence of yourself concerning the matter charged, the Court hath given me command to let you know they will hear you.

CHARLES: Since I see that you will not hear anything of debate concerning that (which I confess) I thought most material for the peace of the kingdom and for the liberty of the subject, I shall waive it; I shall speak nothing to it. Only I must tell you that, this many a day, all things have been taken from me but that is much dearer to me than my life, which is my conscience and my honour. And if I had a respect to my life more than the peace of the kingdom and the liberty of the subject, certainly I should have made a particular defence of myself, for by that at least I might have delayed an ugly sentence which I believe will be passed upon me. Therefore, sir, as a man that hath some understanding, some knowledge of the world, I should have gone to work another way than I have done if my true zeal for my country had not overborne my care for my own preservation.

Now, sir, I conceive that a hasty sentence once passed may sooner be repented of than recalled. I desire before sentence be given that I may be heard in the Painted Chamber before the Lords and the Commons. This delay cannot be long. This delay cannot be prejudicial to you, whatever I may say. If what I say has no reason in it, those that hear me can judge it so. If it has reason and is really for the welfare of the kingdom and the liberty of the subject, then it is surely well worth hearing. Therefore I do conjure you, as you love what you pretend to love (I hope it is real)—the liberty of the subject and the peace of the kingdom—that you will grant me this hearing before any sentence be passed. I only desire this—that you will take this into your consideration. It may be that you have not heard of it beforehand. If you wish, I will retire and you may think of it. But if I cannot have this liberty, then I do protest that your fair words of liberty and peace are rather specious shows than otherwise and that you will not hear your King.

BRADSHAWE: Sir, you have now spoken what you wished?

CHARLES: Yes, sir.

BRADSHAWE: And, sir, what you have said is nothing but a further declining the jurisdiction of this Court, which was the point in which you were limited before.

(*Immediately behind Bradshawe, there is a movement and a whisper.*)

DOWNES: Have we hearts of stone? Are we men?

WALTON: Be quiet, Downes.

DOWNES: I shall protest.

WALTON: You will ruin yourself and the Cause. Keep quiet!

DOWNES: I don't care. I——

CHARLES: Excuse me, sir; I pray you excuse me, sir. You do mistake me. You say a declining of jurisdiction. It is not a declining. It is not, I assure you, sir. You judge me before you hear me speak. It is not a declining of it, since I say that if I do not say anything that is for the peace of the kingdom and the liberty of the subject, then the shame is mine.

DOWNES (*His voice a little above a whisper*): The shame is ours.

CROMWELL: What ails you? Are you mad, Downes? Sit still and be quiet!

DOWNES: Sir, I cannot be quiet. (*In a loud voice to the Hall.*) I, John Downes, a Commissioner of this Court, am not satisfied to give my consent to this sentence, but have reasons to offer you against it. And I desire the Court may adjourn to hear me.

BRADSHAWE: If any of the Court be unsatisfied, the Court must adjourn.

CHARLES: Shall I withdraw?

BRADSHAWE: Sir, you shall know the pleasure of the Court presently. The Court withdraws for half an hour into the Court of Wards. Serjeant-at-arms, the Court gives command that the prisoner be withdrawn until they give the order for his return again.

In the Court of Wards

BRADSHAWE: Now, Colonel Downes, what have you to say?

DOWNES: My Lord President, I should have been glad if the King had made the offer he now makes a long time before this; glad of it both for his sake and for ours. But, sir, for me they are welcome now and not too late. God knows I desire not the King's death but his life. All I want is the settlement of the nation in peace. His Majesty now offers that and asks to make the offer to his Parliament. Should you give sentence of death on him before you have acquainted Parliament with his offer, in my humble opinion your case will be so much altered that I do not know how ever you will be able to answer it.

CROMWELL: My Lord President, you see what weighty reasons this gentleman hath produced to justify all the trouble he has put us to. Surely this gentleman is not so innocent as not to know that with Charles Stuart he is dealing with the hardest-hearted man on earth. Surely he should know. He was once in the King's service. However, sir, it is not the single opinion of one peevish, tenacious man that must sway the Court or deter them from their duty in this great business. And whatever reasons he pretends for his dissatisfaction, he is only trying to save his old master. Therefore, sir, I pray you lose no more time, but get back to the Court and do your duty.

DOWNES: But I am not alone in this?

CROMWELL: Let us see who is with you. Call them! Call them!

DOWNES: I had thought that Sir John Bourchier—Mr. Dixwell—Mr. Love—Mr. Waite?

CROMWELL: Not one. But all of us can tell you how we estimate you. Let me begin. You yourself deserve judgment, since all you aim at is making a mutiny in the Army.

ANOTHER: And let me say that generations to come will curse you for this action of yours.

ANOTHER: If you were in your right wits, you would never have made this interruption; but we all know that your head is weak and you should be rather in Bedlam than here. . . .

(*General laughter.*)

ANOTHER: Well, he's gone.

ANOTHER: And in tears.

CROMWELL: We can better spare him and any waverers. If any of you gentlemen whose names be called—I will not inquire why, that is for God to judge—if any of you would withdraw from our action, let him stay here. The rest of us, gentlemen, back to our great work.

BRADSHAWE: And I am to say to the King——

CROMWELL: Nothing is altered, my Lord President; you will proceed as we have already agreed.

Sentence on the King

BRADSHAWE: Prisoner at the bar, the return I have to you from the Court is this; that they have been too much delayed by you already; that they are judges appointed by the highest authority; and that judges are no more to delay than to deny justice. There must be no delay and therefore, notwithstanding what you have offered, they are resolved to proceed to sentence and judgment and that is their unanimous resolution.

CHARLES: Sir, I know it is vain for me to dispute. I am no sceptic for to deny the power you have. I know that you have power enough. As for this delay I have desired, I confess it is a delay. But it is a delay very important for the peace of the kingdom. I confess I have been here now, I think, a week—this day eight days was the day I came here first. But a little delay of a day or two further may give peace, whereas a hasty judgment may bring on trouble to the kingdom that the child that is unborn may repent of it. And therefore, again, out of the duty I owe God and my country, I do desire that I may be heard by the Lords and Commons in the Painted Chamber or otherwise else you shall appoint. I doubt not but I shall give some satisfaction to all here and my people after that. And therefore I do require you, as you will answer it at the dreadful Day of Judgment, that you will consider it once again.

BRADSHAWE: Sir, I receive direction from the Court. And they will proceed to sentence, if you have nothing more to say.

CHARLES: I have nothing more to say. But I shall desire that this may be entered that I have said.

BRADSHAWE: The Court then, sir, hath something to say unto you which, although I know it will be very unacceptable, yet notwithstanding they are willing and are resolved to do their duty. We cannot be unmindful of what the Scripture tells us "for to acquit the guilty is of equal abomination as to condemn the innocent." We may not acquit the guilty. What sentence the law affirms to a traitor, tyrant, a murderer and a public enemy to the country, that sentence you are now to hear read unto you; and that is the sentence of the Court.

CLERK: Whereas the Commons of England assembled in Parliament have by their late Act instituted 'An Act of the Commons of England for erecting of a High Court of Justice for the trying and judging of Charles Stuart, King of England' authorized and constituted an High Court of Justice for trying and judging of the said Charles Stuart, now upon serious and mature deliberation of the premises and consideration had of the notoriety of the matters of fact charged upon him as aforesaid, this Court, is in judgment and conscience satisfied that he, the said Charles Stuart, is guilty of levying war against the said Parliament and People and of maintaining and continuing the same, for which in the said charge he stands accused; and by the general course of his government, counsels and practices, before and since this Parliament began (which have been and are notorious and public and the effects whereof remain abundantly on record). This Court is fully satisfied in their judgment and consciences that he hath been, and is, guilty of wicked designs and that the said war hath been levied, maintained and continued by him in prosecution and for the accomplishment of the said designs. And that he hath been and is the occasioner, author and continuer of the said unnatural, cruel and bloody wars and therein guilty of High Treason and of the murders, rapines, burnings, spoils, desolations and mischief to this nation, acted and committed in the said war and occasioned thereby. For all which treasons and crimes this Court doth adjudge that the said Charles Stuart, as a tyrant, traitor, murderer and public enemy to the good people of this nation, shall be put to death by severing of his head from his body.

BRADSHAWE: This sentence now read and published, is it the act, sentence, judgment and resolution of the whole Court?

THE COURT: Aye! All! All!

CHARLES: Will you hear me a word, sir?

BRADSHAWE: Sir, you are not to be heard after the sentence.

CHARLES: No, sir?

BRADSHAWE: No, sir; by your favour, sir. Guard, withdraw your prisoner.

CHARLES: I may speak after the sentence—By your favour, sir, I may speak after the sentence. By your favour—hold—the sentence, sir—I say, sir, I do—I am not suffered to speak. Expect what justice other people will have.

(II) The King Prepares for Death

The Farewells to the Family

"As the King was passing after sentence to his lodging, there was a great cry for execution. Entering the house, one of the servants departed weeping, which he seeing said: 'You may forbid their attendance, not their tears.' That night he commanded his dogs should be taken away and sent to his wife, as not willing to have anything present that might take him off from serious consideration of himself. The King now bidding farewell to the world, his whole business was a serious preparation for death, which opens the door into Eternity; in order thereunto he laid aside all other thoughts and spent the remainder of his time in prayer and other pious exercises of devotion, and in conference with the meek and learned Bishop, Juxon, who, under God, was a great support to him in that his afflicted condition; and resolving to sequester himself so as he might have no disturbance to his mind nor interruption to his meditations, he ordered Mr. Herbert to any that might have the desire to visit him."

CHARLES: I know my nephew, the Prince-Elector, will endeavour it and some Lords that love me, which I would take in good part, but my time is short and precious and I am desirous to improve it the best I may in preparation: I hope they will not take it ill that none have access unto me but my children. The best office they can do now is to pray for me.

"And it fell out accordingly; for his Electoral Highness, accompanied by the Duke of Richmond, the Lord Marquis of Hertford, the Earls of Southampton and Lindsey, with some more, having got leave, came to the bed-chamber door, where Mr. Herbert acquainted them with what the King gave him in charge, wherein they acquiesced and, presenting their humble duty to His Majesty, with their prayers, they returned with hearts full of sorrow. The Prince also, then in Holland, by the States Ambassadors interceded with the Parliament and used all possible means with the Army to prevent, or at least to defer the execution."

The Prince of Wales, in an endeavour to save his father's life, had sent to Parliament a blank sheet of paper with his signature attached, so that they might fill in their own conditions.

On Sunday, the Bishop preached privately before the King from the text: "At that day when God shall judge the secrets of men by Jesus Christ." He insisted that, although God's judgments are often deferred, yet they are inescapable. Everything said and done by every man will be subject to the strictest examination. "Yes," said Juxon, "the most hidden things and imaginations of men will most certainly appear at the Day of Judgment, when the Lord Jesus Christ shall be upon His High Tribunal: all designs, though concealed in this life, shall then be plainly discovered."

The Bishop then proceeded to apply the text to the King's present circumstances; to urge the necessity of self-knowledge for himself; to suggest that, behind his enemies' mask of religious zeal, there might be less reputable motives.

Charles had at intervals in the last few days, endeavoured to set down for his eldest son the things that had fallen out as he in honesty saw them. The very long letter, which was his *apologia*, he finished after the service was over, bearing in mind the Bishop's sermon.

At five o'clock in the afternoon he was removed from Whitehall to St. James's, so that he should spend his last two nights undisturbed by the sounds of the carpenters erecting his scaffold. The guards, who on previous nights, had stayed talking and smoking in his bedroom and preventing him sleeping, were withdrawn.

In the evening he gave Herbert a ring—an emerald set between two diamonds—with instructions to go with it to a certain house in Westminster and give it to the lady of the house, without saying anything. Herbert did as he was commanded and brought back the little cabinet which the lady gave him in exchange for the ring.

"Morning being come, the Bishop was early with the King, and after prayers His Majesty broke the seals open and showed them what was contained in it. There were diamonds and jewels, most part broken Georges and Garters."

CHARLES: You see all the wealth now in my power to give my two children.

His two children, Elizabeth, aged thirteen, and Henry, Duke of Gloucester, aged ten, had for six years been brought up as prisoners of Parliament in loneliness and seclusion. When Charles had been allowed to see them again eighteen months before, Cromwell, watching the reunion, had burst into tears. Now they were brought for the last time to take farewell of their father.

"This was the 29th of January. The Princess, being the elder, was the most sensible of her royal father's condition, as appeared by her sorrowful look and excessive weeping and her little brother, seeing his sister weep, he took the like impression, though, by reason of his tender age, he could not have the like apprehension. The King raised them both from off their knees; he kissed them, gave them his blessing, and setting them on his knees, admonished them concerning their duty and loyal observance to the Queen their mother, the Prince that was his successor, love to the Duke of York and his other relations. The King then gave them all his jewels, save the George he wore; and again kissing his children, had such pretty and pertinent answers from both, as drew tears of joy and love from his eyes."

CHARLES: Elizabeth, sweetheart, although I have not time to say much, yet I have something to say to you, which I could not leave in writing. You are not to grieve or torment yourself for me, for it will be a glorious death I shall die, for it is for the laws and liberties of this land. I have forgiven all my enemies and I hope God will forgive them also. And you and all the rest of your brothers and sisters must forgive them. Tell your mother that my thoughts have never strayed from her and that my love for her will be the same to the last. Tell your brother James whenever you see him that it was his father's last desire that he should look on your brother Charles not only as his eldest brother but as his sovereign. And you, too, must remember that. Sweetheart, you'll forget all this.

ELIZABETH: No, I shall never forget it while I live. I will write it down as soon as . . . as soon as . . . I leave you. . . .

(*She breaks into uncontrollable sobs.*)

CHARLES: There, sweetheart, do not grieve. I have told you: it is a glorious death they are giving me. Henry.

HENRY: Yes, Father.

CHARLES: They are going to cut off your father's head. Mark, child, what I say, they will cut off my head and perhaps make you a King. But, mark what I say, you must never be King while your brothers Charles and James are alive. For they will cut off your brothers' heads, when they can catch them; and cut off your head too, at the last. And so I charge you: you must never let them make you King.

HENRY: I will be torn in pieces first.

CHARLES: God will, never doubt, provide for you all. He will settle the throne upon your brother Charles, and you will all live happier than you could have expected if I had lived.

ELIZABETH: No. . . . No. . . . Father!

"Praying God Almighty to bless them, he turned about, expressing a tender and fatherly affection. Most sorrowful was this parting, the young Princess shedding tears and crying lamentably, so as moved others to pity that formerly were hard-hearted; and at opening the bedchamber door the King returned hastily from the window and kissed them and blessed them; so parted."

Cromwell's difficulties

Meanwhile, at Whitehall, Cromwell was experiencing some difficulty in obtaining enough signatures to the King's death-warrant to give at least the appearance of some unanimity among the judges. When the members of the Court were also members of Parliament, Cromwell called on them to sign without further delay.

CROMWELL: Those that are gone in, I will have their hands to it. I will have their hands now.

Later the warrant lay for signature on the table of the Painted Chamber. Cromwell dragged one man to the table and held his hand with the pen and 'marked him in the face with it.' When the man retaliated by spattering ink in his face, Cromwell burst into excited laughter.

CROMWELL: I see you, sir; I have you; though you have escaped me all the while, you shall now sign that paper as well as the rest of us.

INGOLDSBY: I will have no part of the business. Let me out from here.

CROMWELL: When you have signed, sir; when you have signed. Here is the pen. Come to it.

Colonel Matthew Tomlinson

That night, after Juxon had left him to go to Sir Henry Hene's house, where he was lodging, the King called Tomlinson, who was technically his gaoler, into his room. He wished to speak to him privately.

Colonel Matthew Tomlinson was thirty-one, one of the younger generation of the Cromwellian colonels. A man of bravery in the field and ability in negotiation, his loyalty to the Cause had never been in doubt, though he was one of the 'Moderates' who had been chosen by Fairfax to hold conversations with the 'Extremists' during the Leveller troubles the year before. When, in the December of 1648, the King had been brought to Windsor, as the first stage of his journey to trial and death, Tomlinson had been put in personal charge of him and made responsible for his safety. Under him were Lieutenant-Colonel Ralph Cobbett and Captain John Merriman, both much further to the 'Left' than Tomlinson, for they had been sent to guard the Army's interests and prevent the King's escape when he was in the Isle of Wight.

It was just before Christmas—less than five weeks ago—that Cromwell had written to the Governor of Windsor Castle: "Colonel Tomlinson and with him Lieutenant-Colonel Cobbett and Captain Merriman are appointed to the charge of the immediate securing of the King's person and for their assistance and furtherance therein you are desired to appoint such guards of foot and to guard the rooms where he and they shall lodge, as they shall desire."

In those five weeks of proximity, the young Colonel had

become the King's friend, and their relationship was a tribute rather to Tomlinson's own nature and character than to the irresistible personal charm which Charles Stuart could exercise when he would. Seeing things at first hand, he had been immediately appalled by his colleagues' behaviour. The King was allowed no privacy from his gaolers, who were accustomed to lounge smoking in his presence—he could not bear tobacco—and civilians made a point of keeping their hats on in his presence. Any small restriction which might annoy the King had been imposed and his requests were seldom granted. All this Tomlinson had changed in the teeth of opposition and innuendo; but still he had found the duty that had been thrust upon him so 'harsh and unpleasing' that he had more than once asked to be relieved of it. In spite of pressure from Cromwell, he had refused to fall in line with his fellow-colonels and serve as one of the Commissioners for the King's trial. When the days of the trial came and the King was moved from Windsor to London, he had been scrupulous to obey the letter of the law and not even enter Westminster Hall.

As soon as Charles came to London, indeed, measures had been taken to counter Tomlinson's kindness. On the excuse that too many people had access to him, a special party of halberdiers, commanded by the fanatical Colonel Francis Hacker, was appointed to St. James's 'for the stricter observing of the guard.' Tomlinson's own authority was not technically infringed nor was his responsibility for the person of the King lessened; but he had to take orders from Hacker each day for the removal of Charles to the scene of his trial. Though Tomlinson accompanied the King from his bedroom in Whitehall to Westminster, it was Hacker's halberdiers who went with them as guard; and Tomlinson took care to emphasize the situation by refusing to go further than Sir Robert Cotton's house where the King rested on the way to the trial. At the house Tomlinson stayed until Charles returned from Westminster Hall. So far he went, but no farther. He never went with him nor saw him in 'that pretended High Court of Justice.'

When the trial was over and sentence passed, Hacker had ordered that two soldiers were to sleep in the King's room until execution was done. At this Tomlinson could no longer contain himself and his energetic protests got the barbarous order reversed. Indeed from that moment he was, at least in spirit, Charles's man. When he had found that the King wished to send Herbert to the house in Channel Row for the casket of jewels, Tomlinson had no scruple whatever in giving Herbert the password which would take him in safety through the redoubled guards round the Palace.

And, on this last evening of his life, Charles turned to Tomlinson for friendship and advice. He called him into his room and discussed the speech he intended to make on the scaffold. He spoke of his burial and asked that the arranging of it should be left to the Duke of Richmond, his faithful courtier, supporter and cousin, whose wife was Buckingham's daughter. That was formal enough, but the personal friendship suddenly submerged the formality. To this grave, courteous young man who, five weeks ago was unknown to him even by name, Charles, who had so little left to give, bequeathed his gold tooth-pick which he always carried in a case in his pocket. And remembering that, on the morrow, it would be Hacker, not Tomlinson, who would take charge of him on the scaffold as he had at the trial, the King made one last request. Would Tomlinson stay with him to the end? Tomlinson promised. Then he withdrew, leaving Charles alone with Herbert.

Colonel Thomas Herbert

Thomas Herbert, though only eleven years older than Matthew Tomlinson, belonged to a different world, for those eleven years carried him back into the slow, peaceful years—as they seemed in retrospect—of King James's reign. Six years younger than Charles, he was yet essentially the King's contemporary. He was also a much-travelled man. After leaving Trinity College, Cambridge, he had, at the age of twenty-one, gone to the East in the company of that eccentric English adventurer, Sir Robert Shirley, who had married a noble Circassian and, settling in Persia, returned to Europe to negotiate alliances on Persia's behalf. Herbert had met Shirley while he was living in London as Persian envoy to James I and, fascinated by Eastern tales, he had managed to get himself attached to the suite of Sir Dodmore Cotton, whom James, in 1627, sent as English Ambassador to Persia. Though Cotton died on the way, Herbert was determined to assuage his thirst for travel and returned home at his leisure by way of Mesopotamia, India, Ceylon and St. Helena. Back in England, he published, at the age of twenty-eight, his *Description of the Persian Monarchy*, which was popular enough to be reprinted and enlarged as *Some Years' Travels into Divers Parts of Asia and Afrique*. He was thus established as a traveller, an author and a courtier when Tomlinson was still in his 'teens.

In the Civil War, however, he took the same side as Tomlinson and, like him, became one of the Colonels trusted by Fairfax. He had fought at the siege of Bristol and was one of the Parliamentary Commissioners for the King's surrender of Oxford. When the Scots, the following year, sold the King, who had taken refuge among them, to the Parliamentarians, all Charles's personal servants were dismissed. Charles, however, had already noticed Herbert among the Parliamentary Commissioners and realised that he stood apart from the rest as a man to be liked and trusted. He therefore asked Parliament to appoint the Colonel as his Groom of the Bedchamber. They agreed and from that time Herbert became his servant and friend—the only servant, except John Joyner, the cook, who was allowed to stay with him to the end.

Throughout the intervening two years—at Hampton Court, in the Isle of Wight, at Hurst, at Windsor and now at Whitehall and St. James's—Herbert had discharged his difficult task faultlessly. His great personal affection and fidelity to the King, combined with an unshaken loyalty to Parliament which had appointed him, gave him a unique position. Though he had known of the various attempts to rescue the King, he had neither connived at them nor betrayed them and, by keeping alike the confidence of King and of Parliament, he was able in the end to do Charles better service than those Royalists whose single-minded enthusiasm led them into a series of abortive plots, which merely embittered relationships.

There was, however, one occasion in the Isle of Wight when Herbert had barely escaped dismissal. Charles was playing bowls at Carisbrooke when suddenly he felt cold and sent Herbert indoors for his cloak. On reaching the King's bedroom, Herbert discovered the Governor of the Castle and another officer searching the room, having managed to gain admission from the Page of the Backstairs by a combination of threats and bribery. "Mr. Herbert, as he was returning to the Green with His Majesty's cloak, gave the Page a sharp rebuke, which the Governor being acquainted with, threatened Mr. Herbert to give him a dismiss for censuring that act of his; and without doubt had expelled him from the Castle, if His Majesty of his goodness had not passed it by, without either reproaching the Governor or taking notice thereof."

Charles had already appreciated Herbert's worth sufficiently to give his captors no excuse to remove him. Increasingly he came to rely on his congenial companionship, and, in the Isle of Wight, their common literary tastes led the King to put Herbert in charge of his books. Edward Fairfax's translation, in heroic verse, of Tasso's *Godfrey of Bulloigne* was one which 'His Majesty much commended.' Spenser's *Faerie Queene* was another favourite among secular books. But Charles, like his father, delighted most in theology and preferred to immerse himself in Andrewes' sermons and Hooker's *Ecclesiastical Polity*, in the works of Dr. Hammond, in Villalpandus upon *Ezekiel*, etc., and Sands' *Paraphrase upon King David's Psalms*. Herbert, on the other hand, was no theologian; but he and the King shared a love of Shakespeare which Charles acknowledged by giving Herbert his copy of the Second Folio of the poet's works, annotated with his own hand.

As the political situation deteriorated and when, after the second Civil War, it became clear that the King was doomed, Herbert's solicitude increased, and the deep reciprocal affection between him and Charles was obvious to all who came in contact with them.

Now, on this last night, the King told Herbert to bring a pallet-bed into his room and sleep by his side. But after he had helped Charles to bed and drawn the bed-curtains upon him and the resplendent counterpane, 'of a rich, thick blue satin, embroidered with gold and silver in a deep border,' he lay staring sleeplessly at the shadows thrown by the great wax night-light in a silver basin. Only when the King's regular, untroubled breathing told him that he was sleeping peacefully did Herbert fall into a fitful, dream-troubled slumber.

THE DAY

(1) Morning

Dawn at St. James's Palace

THE King woke at about half-past five. Drawing aside his bed-curtains to call Herbert, he noticed that he was disturbed, apparently in the throes of a dream. After he had awakened him, he asked what the dream was.

"May it please your Majesty," said Herbert, "I was dreaming that, as you were making ready, some one knocked at the bedchamber door. Your Majesty took no notice of it and I did not want to call your attention to it, as I thought it might be Colonel Hacker. There was a second knock and Your Majesty asked me if I had not heard it. I said that I had, but that I should not answer it unless you ordered me to. Then Your Majesty said to me: 'Why, then, go and see who it is and find out their business.' "

"Was it Hacker?" asked Charles.

"No, sir. It was Dr. Laud. He was dressed in the pontifical habit that he used to wear at Court when he was Archbishop of Canterbury. I knew him at once, for I often saw him in the old days. He asked if he might see you and when I acquainted Your Majesty with his request, you bade me admit him. After he had entered, he made his obeisance to your Majesty in the middle of the room and then again when he was near you. He fell on his knees as you gave him your hand to kiss. Then you took him aside to the window, where you had a long conversation."

"About what?" asked Charles.

"I kept a becoming distance, sir, and heard nothing that was said. But I noticed that you were looking very thoughtful and that the Archbishop was sighing. After a short stay, he again kissed your hand and left the room, facing Your Majesty all the way. He made the usual reverences, but the third was so low and submissive that he fell flat on his face on the ground. Immediately I went to him to help him up. That was what I was doing when Your Majesty saw me troubled in my sleep. The impression was so vivid that, when you woke me, I looked round for the Archbishop. I could not believe it was only a dream."

"It was indeed a remarkable dream," said the King.

Archbishop Laud had been beheaded four years before on just such a January morning as this, after four years imprisonment in the Tower. The choleric little man with the red face and a passion for order equalled only by his tactlessness, might almost be held to be responsible for the King's present plight. Had he not endeavoured to force the English Prayer Book on the Scots there would not have been that 'Bishop's War' which had forced Charles to call Parliament after an eleven-year interval, and so had led, by inescapable stages, to the Civil War. But the mistake was past undoing now; Laud had atoned for his miscalculations, but even at the time, the King had not always agreed with his Archbishop.

"But he is dead," said Charles. "Yet had we conferred together during his life, 'tis very likely—albeit I loved him well—I should have said something to him that might have occasioned his sigh."

But whatever Laud's errors, there was one thing for which Charles could never be grateful enough. When he took the Archbishopric, he had urged the appointment of William Juxon as his successor as Bishop of London and in that capacity Juxon would now be by Charles's side to the last.

Juxon, nine years younger than Laud, was, like him essentially an Elizabethan, an 'elder statesman' who had grown to manhood in the old Queen's reign. A Londoner, educated at the Merchant Taylor's School and St. John's College, Oxford, he had become vicar of St. Giles, Oxford, in the very early days of King James's reign, when Laud was President of St. John's. He eventually succeeded Laud in that Presidency and was brought by his patron to the King's notice, at the beginning of the 'thirties. "Dr. Juxon," Laud noted in his diary, "was at my suit sworn clerk of His Majesty's closet, that I might have one that I might trust near His Majesty, if I grow weak or infirm."

Whatever the purpose of the appointment, Charles soon grew to like Juxon for himself. Apart from his quiet charm and his exceptional honesty, he had tastes in common with the King. For one thing, he was a passionate lover of hunting and kept a good pack of hounds "and had them so well ordered and hunted, and chiefly by his own skill and direction, that they exceeded all other hounds in England for the pleasure and orderly hunting of them." Also, in spectacular contrast to Laud, "he had as much command of his temper as of his hounds."[1] Juxon was also a connoisseur of architecture and during his tenure of the see of London he undertook the restoration of St. Paul's Cathedral, with Inigo Jones as the designer.

The test of Juxon's character had come in 1636 when Charles had appointed him Lord Treasurer. From every quarter there was indignant anger that the post had been given to an ecclesiastic—a thing unprecedented since the days of King Henry VI. On the Royalist side, the appointment was resented by Juxon's secular rivals for the post and their supporters as prejudicing 'the nobility and the governing houses'; the Puritans saw it as but another flagrant instance of the intention of the King and the Archbishop to erect an absolute tyranny by controlling secular affairs

[1] Throughout the days of the Commonwealth, during which he lived in retirement at his house in Warwickshire, he continued to hunt with enthusiasm. On one occasion his hounds followed a fast scent through Chipping Norton churchyard at the time of a Puritan service. The worshippers appealed to Cromwell against the outrage, but the Protector, who was also a sportsman, dismissed their complaint as frivolous and ruled that as long as the Bishop did not disturb his government he was free to enjoy his hunting.

through the Church, without reference to Parliament—which had already been dispensed with for eight years. But Juxon, who was the only honest Lord Treasurer of the century, had by his conduct and his character forced a reversal of the hasty judgment. When the troubles came and the Long Parliament had ordered the impeachment of Laud and condemned the whole episcopal order, Juxon alone was, by name, exempted from the attack. Even the waspish Prynne, in his scurrilous attack on the episcopate, *The Antipathy of the English Lordly Prelacy both in Regal Monarchy and Civil Unity*, felt bound to say of Juxon that "his disposition and carriage as a man have been amiable and commendable."

Juxon was now sixty-six. As the one man about him older than himself, Charles increasingly turned to him for strength and comfort quite apart from his office, and in this crisis of his fate Juxon was more to him than Laud could ever have been. He had asked him to come early to the palace, so that he might spend as long with him as possible before going to Whitehall. And, as he also wished to dress carefully for the occasion, Charles decided that he must start his toilet now, though it still needed two hours to sunrise.

"I will get up now," he said to Herbert, "for I have a great work to do to-day. Herbert, I would be as trim to-day as may be. It is my second marriage-day, for before night I hope to be espoused to my blessed Jesus."

He chose his clothes carefully. It was bitterly cold—so bitter that the Thames was frozen over—and he decided to put on an extra shirt, lest he might shiver and give the spectators the impression that he was trembling. "I would have no imputation of fear," he said to Herbert. "I do not fear death. Death is not terrible to me. I bless my God I am prepared."

Herbert selected two linen shirts, one, open down the front, and embroidered on the collar, sleeves and round the lower edges with open work, with small bows of red and blue ribbon; the other, with embroidered ruffles and a very broad collar. The waistcoat Charles decided to wear was a rich red striped silk, brocaded with silver and yellow. It matched the skull-cap of crimson silk embroidered with gold which he usually wore but which he had sent 'as the only token and remembrance he could bestow' to 'his highly esteemed friend and faithful servant,' Colonel William Salusbury, a seventy-year old knight who had raised a Welsh regiment for him in the war and, as Governor of Denbigh Castle, had held out against an exceptionally long siege.

The cap that Charles chose for the scaffold and entrusted now to Herbert's keeping was of unlined linen, with the edge turned up so as to form a deep border. It was exquisitely embroidered, worked all over with scrolls of gilt thread, enclosing flowers and fruit of raised silk, roses, honeysuckles, grapes and mulberries—a symbol of summer.

For the rest, he would dress in black—though, as he emphasized to Herbert, 'not in mourning.' His black satin doublet and breeches, and his short velvet cloak, would be relieved only by the blue of the Garter ribbon, his 'George' and the Garter itself, which glittered with four hundred and twelve small diamonds. His ear-rings should be those he usually wore, each a single pearl surmounted by a small gold crown.

Charles's long chestnut hair was now streaked with white and he had grown careless of its appearance. His beard, which it had been his custom to wear 'picked,' he had allowed to grow naturally for the last year—since the 'Vote of No Addresses'[1]—and here too its unaccustomed fulness

[1] The 'Vote of No Addresses,' which meant an end of the Army's negotiation with the King, was passed in the January of 1648. Whatever may be the truth about Charles' purported autobiographical memoir *Eikon Basilike* (and I see no reason to doubt that, whoever may have edited it, it is essentially his own work), there can be little doubt of the authenticity of the opening of the last chapter, set down *After the Vote of No Addresses and His Majesty's closer imprisonment in Carisbrooke Castle*: "As I have leisure enough, so I have cause more than enough to meditate on and prepare for my death: for I know there are but few steps between the prisons and graves of Princes." From this moment, Charles seems to have taken little interest in his personal appearance.

made the white very apparent. But to-day he must be barbered with the greatest attention. "Though it has not long to stand on my shoulders, take all the care you can of my head," he said to Herbert, as he opened the ebony and silver dressing-case, with its ivory powder-box, its shaving-brush, its three combs—one silver, one tortoiseshell, one wood—and its scissors. This was part of being 'as trim to-day as may be.'

The long, careful toilet continued till dawn and at eight o'clock as the sun rose, Dr. Juxon arrived, punctually as he had promised, bringing with him a chalice[1] and a paten and bread and wine.

Business at Westminster

In the House of Commons

At eight o'clock, the House of Commons assembled for the ordinary business of the day, but St. Stephen's Chapel, which could be so uncomfortably crowded when its five tiers of benches were full, had so sparse an attendance that its comparative emptiness emphasized the cold rawness of the day.

After Prayers, the Speaker presented to the House, in the form of an official report, a letter which had been sent to him personally the previous day. It was from the Ambassadors of the States General of the United Netherlands, Albert Joachimi, who was resident in London, and Adrian Pauw, Ambassador Extraordinary, who had arrived a few days before expressly to intercede for the life of the King.

Pauw, from the moment of his arrival, had been under no illusions about the failure of his mission. He and Joachimi had seen Fairfax and asked for a private audience. The Lord General had taken them into his private room, but hardly

[1] The chalice from which Charles received Holy Communion that morning bears on it the arms of Sir Henry Hene, at whose house Juxon was lodging at the time. It was lent by the Duke of Portland to the Exhibition of Relics belonging to the Royal House of Stuart held in London in 1889.

The King on the Scaffold and the Execution of the Regicides

THE CONFESSION OF Richard Brandon

The Hangman (upon his Death-bed) concerning His beheading his late Majesty, CHARLES the first, King of Great Brittain; and his Protestation and Vow touching the same; the manner how he was terrified in Conscience; the Apparitions and Visions which apeared unto him; the great judgment that befell him three dayes before he dy'd; and the manner how he was carryed to White-Chappell Church-yard on Thursday night last, the strange Actions that happened thereupon; With the merry conceits of the Crowne Cook and his providing mourning Cords for the Buriall.

Printed in the year Year, of the Hang-mans down-fall, 1649.

Title-page of pseudo-Royalist satire on the Hangman

(*By courtesy of the British Museum, London*)

had they started to talk when Cromwell had burst in accompanied by other officers, neither asking for admission nor apologizing for the intrusion. The officers were there as witnesses when Fairfax opened the Letters of Credence, which neither he nor Cromwell would open alone. This was the less surprising since, as Pauw reported to the States General, neither Fairfax nor Cromwell dared go about without a guard of three hundred horse. It was obvious that nothing would be done, but the Ambassadors had followed the correctitude of procedure enjoined on them by writing formally to the Speaker. And now Bradshawe, on his part, had equally correctly, had the letter embodied in a Report.

As Cromwell and Ireton and Harrison and the rest of those who had signed the King's death warrant were all in the House—quite apart from the fact that the House itself had now the appearance of a Revolutionary Committee—there was little debate. It was ordered that the Ambassador's plea should be referred to a Committee to prepare and present to the House an Answer, with reasons, to why the House "did not think fit to stay the Proceedings of the Court of Justice." The 'Committee' was to consist of two, Ireton and Henry Marten, the stern, unbending Republican—with Oldisworth, Challoner, Scott and Robinson to choose from as alternatives if the more famous principals were otherwise engaged. They were to draft the reply that afternoon.

By then the *fait accompli* would have made the answer irreversible. On the other hand, no one wished to antagonize the Ambassadors more than was necessary. Indeed, friendly relations with Holland were likely to be more than ever necessary, in view of the general European reactions to the day's work. So the House decided to entertain Joachimi and Pauw as well as possible and voted a sum of five hundred pounds to be paid to their steward for that purpose.

There were one or two other payments to sanction. Thomas Parker, the Usher of the Queen's Court—where the

Committees of the House sat—had ten pounds for out-of-pocket expenses; and the official Printer to the House, Edward Husbands, having presented a bill for seven hundred and nineteen pounds and sixpence, owing to him, was given two hundred pounds at once, with a promise of the remainder in quarterly instalments. These were routine business, but a third payment had a seasonable urgency, as Members sat there shivering in the half-light of the grey morning. The House ordered "that two hundred pounds *per annum* be allowed to Edward Birkhead, Esquire, Sergeant-at-Arms attending this House, to make provisions of wood, coals, candles, torches and other necessaries." The payment was to be made in the form of fifty pounds each Quarter Day, but in view of present conditions, it was additionally ordered that "the first payment commence from the 29th of September last." The House was, indeed, freezing. Ireton and Harrison were so cold that, as soon as the proceedings were over, they rushed back to Whitehall and got into bed together to try to warm themselves.

Before the House adjourned, however, there were one or two other matters to attend to. First in importance, the Prince Elector, Charles Louis, was given permission to see the King. Such an interview would be perfectly safe. Charles Louis, the King's nephew, Prince Rupert's elder brother, had for years taken the Puritan side. He had spent some years in England as an exile from his own throne and had periodically pestered Cromwell to use the Parliamentary Army on the Continent to fight for the restoration of his rights. In the English contest between Parliament and Army, he had always been noticed to veer to whichever side seemed for the moment in the ascendant; and nobody placed much reliance on him. But now that the 'Thirty Years War' was over (it had been concluded by the treaty of Westphalia the previous year) and Charles Louis had been restored to at least some part of his inheritance, Cromwell thought it as well to humour him. It was for his sake that the permission to see the King was granted, not for the sake of Charles himself, who had little affection for his eldest nephew and had already announced that he did not wish to see him.

The remainder of the morning's business was of a congratulatory nature. Among the members of the House were Colonel John Hutchinson, who had held Nottingham for Parliament and was Governor of the town and castle as well as M.P. for the shire. Hutchinson's wife, Lucy, brother of Sir Allen Apsley, the Royalist governor of Exeter, put it on record (in those *Memoirs* which were to make Colonel Hutchinson one of the most vivid characters of the century for posterity) that he sat as a Commissioner for the trial of the King "very much against his own will; but looking upon himself as called hereunto durst not refuse it, as holding himself obliged by the covenant of God and the public trust of his country reposed in him."

One of the most honourable of the King's opponents, Hutchinson was not at all intimidated by Cromwell but followed his own judgment. "Being called to an extraordinary action, whereof many were of several minds, he addressed himself to God by prayer; desiring the Lord that, if through any human frailty he were led into any error or false opinion in these great transactions, He would open his eyes and not suffer him to proceed, but that He would confirm his spirit in the truth and lead him by a right, enlightened conscience; and, finding no check, but a confirmation in his conscience that it was his duty to act as he did he, upon serious debate, both privately and in his addresses to God, and in conferences with conscientious, upright, unbiassed persons, proceeded to sign the sentence against the King."

Of a very different nature was his fellow-M.P. for Nottingham, the weak and shifty Gilbert Millington, who had shown himself strident in his demands for the King's execution; but though Hutchinson had reason enough to complain of Millington's deceitful and dishonourable conduct with regard to himself, he recognized him, at this moment, as a brother in the Cause. Nor did their constituents distinguish between them and when a message, approving of the regicidal course taken by Parliament from 'divers well-affected persons in Nottingham' was read, the official reply was, with equal correctitude, entrusted to them both. The House ordered "that Colonel Hutchinson and Mr. Millington be desired to return thanks, from this House, to the petitioners, for their good affections and expressions set forth in their petition."

Another of those who had been a commissioner for the trial and a signatory of the death-warrant was Captain Fry; but as his constituents were no further away than Southwark, they came in person, headed by one, Thomas Prince, to stand at the bar of the House to express their satisfaction and present a petition.

When the morning's proceedings were at last over, and the House adjourned till the afternoon, Richard Nunnelly, who was the door-keeper to the Committee of the Army, came up to Cromwell to deliver to him a warrant for fifty thousand pounds.

"Are you going to Whitehall?" asked Cromwell.

Nunnelly hesitated.

"Surely you are coming to see the beheading of the King?" insisted Oliver, incredulous that any should wish to be absent. And without more ado he took Nunnelly with him and let him into Whitehall by the private entrance.

In the House of Lords

The attendance in the House of Lords that morning had sunk to five—Denbigh (who acted as Speaker), Pembroke, Mulgrave, Kent and Grey. Their business, apart from the formal summoning of all the Lords and the Judges to attend the House on Thursday two days hence, was ecclesiastical and short.

It concerned the Petition of Zachary Cawdrey, a Fellow of St. John's, Cambridge. This energetic and uncompromising young man of thirty-two had for the last two years, been a thorn in the Puritan flesh. Not only had he persisted in reading services from the proscribed Book of Common Prayer and in using a ring in marriage and the sign of the Cross in baptism, but he had refused to obey a House of Lords' order prohibiting him to continue these practices. Moreover he had protested against the obedience of the Master and the other Fellows in these matters. As if this were not enough, he had then actually prayed in the College chapel for the success of the Royal cause and for confusion to the King's enemies, as well as showing his sympathy in the practical form of a contribution to Charles's treasury. As a warning punishment, the House of Lords had deprived him of his Proctorship.

Cawdrey, quite unabashed, was now petitioning "that by sentence of this House he was put out of the Proctorship of the University of Cambridge; but the said sentence hath, by the petitioner's adversaries, been enlarged not only to the taking away of the Proctorship, but likewise to the depriving him of his seniority in the College, and much of his due emolument and all College preferments."

This was a serious matter, as Denbigh, himself a Cambridge man, realized. The injustice was immediately remedied by a formal declaration: ". . . the Lords in Parliament assembled do declare that their intentions were, by the said Order, only to extend to the Proctorship; and not to put any other incapacity upon him, the said Zachary Cawdrey, for any other preferment in the University."[1]

[1] Zachary Cawdrey's anti-Puritanism was inherited by his more famous grandson, Zachary Grey, the anti-Nonconformist writer who annotated the edition of *Hudibras* illustrated by Hogarth.

To dispel any suspicion of sympathy with Cawdrey's theological point of view, the Lords then ordered the institution and induction of a Nonconformist to a Crown living in Lincolnshire, and, having thus transacted their outstanding business adjourned till ten o'clock on Thursday.

In the Painted Chamber

The immediate arrangements of the day however, were discussed neither in the Commons nor in the Lords but by the Commissioners for the trial and execution sitting in the Painted Chamber.

This historic room, which was normally used as a place of conference between Lords and Commons jutted out at right-angles at the lower end of the House of Lords. Its foundation walls were still those of St. Edward the Confessor's original palace and the room itself was said to have been his bed-chamber, where he died. Its name, however, referred not to its pre-Norman days but to its rebuilding and redecoration by King Henry III when its walls were covered by paintings of the wars of the Maccabees and other Old Testament exploits, as well as episodes from the hagiography of the Confessor. The fame of it was such that two Franciscans, travelling from Ireland to Jerusalem in the fourteenth century, had noted above all else, during their passage through London, "the well-known Chamber on whose walls all the histories of the wars of the whole Bible are painted beyond description (*ineffabiliter depictae*), with most complete and perfect inscriptions in French."

But, after the Reformation, the Protestants were interested neither in the Apocrypha (which they excluded from the Bible) nor in the lives of the Saints (whose statues they destroyed) and for a century now the splendid paintings had been covered with whitewash. The consequent bareness of the walls had been relieved by tapestries, which so far acknowledged tradition that their subject was still military —the Trojan War in five scenes—while the original ceiling, ornamented with the gilded and painted tracery and small wainscot paterae that were so novel four centuries earlier, formed a link with the splendid past.

Throughout the King's trial the Commissioners had met in private here; and here they had signed the death-warrant. Now at nine o'clock in the morning they had one or two last points to clear up before the event for which they had been constituted and after which they could disband.

First, they ordered that the railings of the scaffold were to be hung with black so that the actual execution would be screened from spectators in the street who would be able to see nothing but the axe swinging high above the hidden block. Secondly, they proceeded to appoint five Puritan divines to visit the King at St. James's.

Three names stood out as inevitable choices. Stephen Marshall, Philip Nye and Joseph Caryl could claim the privilege almost as of right. Taken together, they might be said to represent the public spirituality of the Cromwellians. At fifty-five, Stephen Marshall was the eldest of them and incomparably the most powerful. Of a middle height, a swarthy complexion and broad shoulders, he had an uncouth, shambling gait and a trick of rolling his eyes about in conversation so that he never looked at the person he was speaking to. He had discovered when he was at Cambridge that he had a gift of pulpit oratory and, at twenty-eight, had been made Vicar of the wealthy parish of Finchingfield in Essex. Considering himself worthy of preferment, he unsuccessfully applied to Buckingham for a deanery and, the refusal rankling, went over to the Puritans, and made himself a kind of father-confessor of the rich manufacturers of the industrial east. By this means he amassed considerable wealth, though he managed to do it with a tact which made him an earlier edition of the Vicar of Bray—"so supple a soul that he brake not a joint, nay, sprained not a sinew in all the alteration of the times."

He soon saw, however, that his securest interest lay on the Parliament side and, when the 1640 elections were being held, he threw himself whole-heartedly into the fray with his sermons. The intense passions he was able to arouse among his hearers made him a political force of such dimensions that, in the opinion of Lord Clarendon, Marshall wielded greater power than Laud himself. Indeed it was said, with some degree of truth that 'if the King had made him a Bishop before he was too engaged' the whole war might have been prevented. As it was, his most famous sermon, *Meroz Cursed*, which he preached up and down the country sixty times, 'ushered in as well as promoted' the conflict.

Though Marshall's private tastes were simple enough—he liked reading himself to sleep over a 'romance'—his demagogy grew by what it fed on. He became fascinated by the sound of his own voice and would sometimes continue an extempore prayer for two hours. It so happened that the King had wounded him in this tender spot. When Marshall was appointed official chaplain to the King in his captivity at Holmby House, Charles had persistently refused to go to hear him preach and, when he had started to declaim an interminable grace at table, Charles would calmly say his own and start his meal while Marshall was still praying.

Philip Nye, two years younger than Marshall, was of a different, if not less dangerous, mould. If Marshall loved money[1] and exhibitionism, Nye loved power. He liked to know all that was going on and move behind the scenes to check or to encourage it. Marshall was, instinctively, one of the great orators of the century while Nye, with an unpleasing voice, tended to irritate his congregations by reading

[1] Marshall died worth £10,000 in the currency of the time—equivalent to about half a million to-day.

his sermons. He was eccentric without being endearing. His 'thanksgiving beard' was unique and looked like 'a tail upon his throat.' A fierce opponent of Anglican ritual, he was a stickler for his own, which consisted of keeping his hat on while he was preaching but taking it off at Holy Communion and insisting that his congregation did the reverse—received Holy Communion sitting with their hats on but uncovering when they listened to him in the pulpit.

Joseph Caryl was, though he had often preached before Parliament, a quieter man than the other two. He had been 'intruded' into the Anglican church of St. Magnus Martyr, by London Bridge, when the Parliamentary victory had meant the outlawing of the Church of England. His main interest was Biblical theology—he spent fifteen years writing a commentary of the Book of Job—but he had unfortunately antagonized the King during his appointment at Holmby, as fellow-chaplain with Marshall.

The other two ministers whom the Commissioners chose to accompany these three notables were a soldier turned preacher, Jonas Dell, usually known as 'the quaking soldier' —a fierce anti-Ritualist whose most popular polemic was *Forms the Pillar of Antichrist, but Christ in spirit the True Teacher of His People*—and Arthur Salway, one of the lesser preachers before the Long Parliament during the Civil War.

Having selected the five, the Commissioners ordered Lieutenant-Colonel Goffe "forthwith to repair unto His Majesty" at St. James's to inform him that the godly ministers were on their way "to administer to him those spiritual helps that should be suitable to his present condition."

Lieutenant-Colonel William Goffe was the obvious man to be in charge of the ministerial band. Religion was in his blood. His elder brother, Stephen, and his second brother, John, were both Anglican divines who had remained constant in their Royalism. Stephen had been one of Charles's trusted chaplains, whom the King had employed in negotiations on the Continent and with the Scots. Now on the verge of conversion to Catholicism, he was to become as a Catholic priest chaplain to Queen Henrietta in Paris. John, who had suffered imprisonment by Parliament for refusing to take the Covenant, remained enthusiastically Anglican and was now living in retirement composing his *Ecclesiae Anglicanae Threnodia.* The family predisposition to religion had, in William, run to an individual extreme of private illumination by the Holy Spirit. Half-crazy with dreams and revelation, he inflicted his apocalyptic visions on his fellow-Roundheads to an extent which had earned him the nickname of 'the praying Colonel,' In situations where Cromwell would summon a Committee, Goffe would call a prayer-meeting. At one moment recently when mundane action was being discussed, Goffe had held up the proceedings while he told his brother officers in considerable detail how he had spent a sleepless night pondering on "the conjunction between Antichrist, or that Mystery of Iniquity, the Church, with Kings and great men." But, in action, Goffe was so fine a soldier that Cromwell could, in a crisis, put him in command of his own regiment.[1] For this, much tedium might be forgiven him and, when absent from the field, he was given whatever congenial employment could be found to satisfy his religious foibles.

As soon as the Commissioners had appointed him, Goffe set off for St. James's to inform the King of the spiritual consolation which had been arranged for him on the verge of death.

[1] At the Restoration, he escaped to Massachusetts and the last glimpse history has of him is fighting Indians. "The town of Hadley was alarmed by the Indians in 1675 in the time of public worship and the people were in the utmost confusion. Suddenly a grave, elderly person appeared in the midst of them. In his mien and dress he differed from the rest of the people. He not only encouraged them to defend themselves, but put himself at their head, rallied, instructed and led them on to encounter the enemy, who by this means were repulsed."

The King's Bequests

When Dr. Juxon entered the King's apartments, Herbert made ready to withdraw, but before leaving the room he fell on his knees and asked Charles's pardon for any negligence he might ever have shown in his duty while he had been in attendance on him. The King gave him his hand to kiss and told him there was nothing to forgive.

Juxon noticed immediately this implication of a status other than that of gaoler and Charles explained to him that, the previous evening, he had given Herbert a certificate written in his own hand which made it quite clear to the world 'that Mr. Herbert was not imposed upon him but was by His Majesty chosen to attend him in his bedchamber and had served him with faithfulness and loyal affection.' Charles was determined that, in the event of a restoration of his house, there should be no mistake about the part that Herbert had played during these last years. If he had no other power left, he could still safeguard his friends—as the gift of the gold toothpick would, he assumed, safeguard Tomlinson also.

Before Herbert left the King and the Bishop alone together for the final easing of Charles's conscience, there were the last gifts to be arranged—the books which the King would not part with and which were still there in the room. Chief among them was the great Bible, in its red velvet binding, richly embroidered with the Royal Arms and other devices in gold and silver thread and coloured silks. In its margins the King had written many annotations and quotations. Always he had been a great reader of the Scriptures and lately he had derived much consolation from the second chapter of *Ecclesiasticus* which Herbert's cousin had drawn his attention to.

Sir Henry Herbert, one-time Master of the Revels and

Gentleman-in-Ordinary to the Privy Chamber, had met Thomas Herbert in St. James's Park and asked him how the King was. When they parted, Sir Herbert had asked Thomas 'to present his humble duty to the King, with an assurance that himself and many others of His Majesty's servants fervently prayed for him and requested that His Majesty would please to read the second chapter of *Ecclesiasticus*; for he would find comfort in it, aptly suiting his present condition.'

Charles on receiving the message had immediately turned to his Bible and read the chapter from its beginning: "My son, if thou come to serve the Lord, prepare thy soul for temptation. Set they heart aright and constantly endure and make not haste in time of trouble. Cleave unto him and depart not away, that thou mayest be increased at thy last end. Whatsoever is brought upon thee, take cheerfully and be patient when thou art changed to a low estate. For gold is tried in the fire, and acceptable men in the furnace of adversity" to its final exhortation: "They that fear the Lord will prepare their hearts and humble their souls in his sight, saying, We will fall into the hands of the Lord and not into the hands of men: for as his majesty is, so is his mercy."

The King now took his Bible and handed it to Herbert, charging him to give it to Prince Charles as soon as he returned to England. He repeated slowly, in front of Juxon, what he had already said to his youngest children and something of what he had already written to his eldest—'that he would be dutiful and indulgent to the Queen, his mother, and affectionate to his brothers and sisters, who were also to be observant and dutiful to him their sovereign.' He insisted that he had forgiven his enemies from his heart and was dying in perfect charity with all men and advised his son 'to exceed in mercy, not in rigour.' Forseeing the danger that Prince Charles, supported by Presbyterian Scotland, might make the same mistake as he had and, for political reasons, seek a compromise with Presbyterianism, the King then made his affirmation of faith in the necessity of Episcopacy: "As for Episcopacy, it is still my opinion that it is of Apostolic institution and, in this kingdom, has been exercised from primitive times; and in this matter, as in all other affairs, I pray God will vouchsafe my son, both in reference to Church and State, a pious and discerning spirit.'[1]

Finally Charles emphasized that 'it was his last and earnest request that the Prince would frequently read the Bible, which in all time of his affliction had been his best instructor and delight; and that he would meditate on what he read.'

To Princess Elizabeth, Charles left his volumes of Dr. Lancelot Andrewes's *Sermons*, Hooker's *Ecclesiastical Polity* and a book which had meant much to him, Archbishop Laud's account of his conferences with the Jesuit, Father John Fisher, in 1622. Father Fisher had converted the old Countess of Buckingham to Catholicism and the Court was buzzing with rumours that Buckingham himself would follow. To avert such an impolitic step, King James had arranged for Laud to engage in a public disputation with Fisher which he and Charles and Buckingham had attended. As a result of Laud's arguments Buckingham had remained settled in 'the true Protestant religion' and fourteen years later, when Charles, King now, was faced by another wave of influential conversions to Catholicism he had ordered Laud to republish the disputation to reinforce his royal proclamation against 'the withdrawing His Majesty's subjects from the Church of England and giving scandal in resorting to masses.' The arguments which made so deep

[1] It is this declaration of faith, with its implicit apology for his 'political' compromises with Presbyterianism at the time of the 'Engagement,' which justified the Church of England in holding that Charles died a martyr for the then fundamental Anglican tenet of the necessity of Bishops in the Apostolical Succession.

and lasting an impression on him, when he heard them in his early twenties, must, Charles had felt, convince all right-minded people.

And nothing, even now, had changed his opinion. As he handed his copy to Herbert to give to his daughter, he remarked to Juxon: "It will ground her against Popery."

To his small son, Henry, Duke of Gloucester, the King left Dr. Hammond's *Practical Catechism* and the voluminous writings of his father, King James.

To his second son, James, Duke of York, a boy of fifteen, who, nine months earlier, had managed to escape to the Continent, Charles did not leave a book—at least, not a theological book. He knew that James was unlikely to read it. The boy preferred outdoor activities and Charles had had to admonish him more than once recently 'to ply his book more and his gun less.' But since the Prince of Wales had been sent to safety abroad, the King in the last year or two had, when he was allowed to see his children, come to rely more and more on James. He had found that he could trust him implicitly, for James (who had been at the battle of Edgehill when he was nine) had a practical wisdom far beyond his years and a gift of keeping his own counsel rare at any age.

So to James the King left a gift which was, in its way, the most personal of all, something which was itself a message of understanding and affection.[1] Charles's own tutor in mathematics, Richard Delamaine, had once written an ingenious treatise entitled *Grammelogia or the Mathematical Ring*. Moreover, he had actually invented and made such a ring for his royal pupil. It was a large ring sundial of silver and could be used 'in resolving many questions of arithmetic' and there were besides 'other rare operations to be

[1] It seems to me probable that James had admired it and that, in their conversations during Charles's captivity, the King would have taught him to use it.

wrought by it in mathematics.' This unique jewel which the King always kept with him and valued greatly, was to go to James, and with it the copy of *Grammelogia*—one book, at least, that the young Duke might find pleasure in reading voluntarily.

There were two other bequests. The Earl of Lindsay, the Lord High Chamberlain, was to have the King's copy of *Cassandra* and his gold watch was to go to the Duchess of Richmond—Buckingham's elder daughter Mary, the 'Little Mall' who had been born in the year that her grandmother 'Great Mall' had by her conversion precipitated the argument between Laud and Fisher.

When the various gifts had been entrusted to Herbert for delivery 'as opportunity served,' the King asked him to withdraw that he might unburden his soul to Juxon. For about an hour, Charles remained 'in private with the Bishop.' At the end of it, Colonel Goffe arrived with the news that spiritual comfort had been appointed for him and announced the names of the five ministers who were preparing to visit him.

Charles replied tersely that "he preferred not to be troubled with them."

Trouble about a Headsman

The question of who should be entrusted with the actual beheading of the King had been exercising the Commissioners' minds for the last two days. There had, of course, been volunteers, but they were for the most part unbalanced nonentities who wished to seize so spectacular a chance of stepping into history. Two of them, indeed, Mathew and Allured, continued for years to boast that they had done it, until at the Restoration they were examined and found to be exhibitionists, not regicides.

Colonel Daniel Axtell and Colonel John Hewson, in

charge of this part of the proceedings, quite properly preferred not to use any of 'the several persons who came and offered themselves out of a kind of zeal to do the thing.' "We did not think it proper," they explained, "to employ persons who we did not know." Consequently Colonel Hewson had called his lieutenant and ordered him to assemble about forty sergeants from three regiments on duty in London—Hacker's, Pride's and Fairfax's—and bring them to him privately.

Thirty-eight had been eventually collected. Hewson had made them swear on the Bible that they would never reveal what he was about to ask them and then offered £100 down and the promise of rapid preferment in the Army to any two who would come forward as volunteers for the post of headsman and headsman's assistant. All the sergeants refused, though not all with the same emphasis.

"Who would not undertake to do this act?" Captain Atkins later asked Sergeant Richard Gittens.

"I would not do it for all the City of London," answered Gittens.

"Neither would I," said Atkins, "for all the world." "But," he added, as if it had no connection with the matter, "you will see that Sergeant Hulet is soon promoted."

But if Sergeant Hulet had shown a certain hesitancy in scorning £100 down and a promise of promotion, Colonel Hewson had, at that point, not taken much notice of it. It was sufficient that he had refused. There were other ways of getting volunteers—the well-tried method, for example, of ordering people to draw lots for any unpleasant duty that had to be done—and there was always the chance that someone of standing, like Hugh Peters, might offer himself. The more immediate necessity, the day before the execution, had been to get the axe.

The Commissioners in the Painted Chamber had ordered "that the Officers of the Ordnance within the Tower of

London, or any other officer or officers of the store within the Tower of London or any other officers within the said Tower in whose hands or custody the bright execution axe for the executing of malefactors is do forthwith deliver unto Edward Dendy, Esquire, Sergeant-at-Arms, attending this Court or his deputy or deputies the said axe." In spite of their vagueness as to where exactly the implement was and who had the right to guard it, it was found and duly delivered to Whitehall. When the execution-morning dawned, the scaffold and the axe were ready. But there was still no executioner.

In the circumstances, it was thought best not to press an unwilling representative of the Army but to have recourse to the common hangman, Richard—commonly known as Gregory—Brandon. Such a choice would make up in effectiveness what it lacked in symbolism and Colonel Daniel Axtell dispatched his brother, Elisha, with an escort of soldiers to take a boat to the Tower and to fetch him and his implement from his house in Whitechapel. They could also bring his official assistant, Ralph Jones, a dustman, who lived near him in the same street, Rosemary Lane.

When Elisha Axtell and his men arrived there, however, they found that Brandon, though obviously terrified by the display of force, refused absolutely to do what was asked of him. He said that he 'would be shot or otherwise killed rather than do it.' His protestations, however, did not save him from being taken, with his 'instruments' which included the little, low block, back to Whitehall. He went alone. Jones could not, at the moment, be found. Nor was it worth while wasting time searching for him, as there would certainly be no difficulty in getting a soldier to perform the assistant's duty of holding up the King's severed head and crying: "Behold the head of a traitor!"

At Whitehall, Elisha Axtell delivered Brandon to his brother Daniel who, with Hewson and others, set about breaking down his resistance. They offered him £200 for the work. He indignantly refused it. Changing their tactics, they threatened him with death by burning. Shaking in body, but still firm in mind, he still refused and reiterated that he would rather die than execute the King. They realized then that it was hopeless. They could, indeed, force him on to the scaffold, but such a course, with him in this mood, would be disastrous. His public reluctance might turn the scale in Charles's favour. Things were dangerous enough as it was.

There had been a report that Downes, who had caused so much trouble at the trial, had now turned completely King's man and was trying to organize a rescue. Worse still, the Lord General Fairfax himself had, at this eleventh hour, declared himself against the execution and had been consulting his own regiment about possible steps to prevent it. Cromwell, as soon as he had returned from the House of Commons, had hastened to take Fairfax in hand. He had suggested that, before the execution, they should hold a prayer-meeting, which the leaders of all sections of opinion should attend, humbly to seek the will of God in the matter and Fairfax, partly from conviction that such a proceeding must issue in the King's safety and partly to gain time, had agreed. The prayer meeting was to begin shortly in a room off the Long Gallery.

In these circumstances, Colonel Daniel Axtell decided to put Brandon under close arrest until the execution was over and, with Colonel Hewson, to select a willing headsman and his assistant. The choice of them, however arrived at, was now urgent. Colonel Francis Hacker, who, with his fellow-Colonels Huncks and Phayre, was in charge of the actual execution, pointed out that the warrant from the Commissioners instructed him "to see the said sentence executed in the open street before Whitehall between the hours of ten in the morning and five in the afternoon" and that it was already nearly ten o'clock.

Hacker also decided that, whatever arrangements might finally be made, it would in any case be safer to bring Charles to Whitehall than to leave him any longer at St. James's. Though he was satisfied that St. James's Park was so well guarded with tried and reliable soldiers that any attempt to rescue was foredoomed to failure, time was on the side of the discontented. Hacker would conduct Charles across the Park at once, while Axtell and Hewson broached the matter once more to Sergeant Hulet.[1]

Meanwhile, in the Banqueting Hall itself, another unofficial conference was held. Richard Nunnelly, having been brought into Whitehall by Cromwell, met in the Long Gallery Cromwell's chaplain Hugh Peters, who took him under his wing and allowed him to accompany him into the Banqueting Hall itself.

Hugh Peters was one of the most influential men of the times. The son of a Dutch refugee and a year older than Cromwell, he had in the 'thirties, after being expelled from Cambridge, and prosecuted by a London butcher for adultery, preached to—on his own estimate—overflowing congregations at St. Sepulchre's, opposite Newgate, where 'above an hundred every week were persuaded from sin to Christ.' After an enforced journey abroad he returned when the troubles started and discovered that his gifts of oratory, combined with a jovial temperament, made him an ideal Army chaplain for the Puritans.

With no convictions, except those that concerned his own comfort, and little theology, this 'very pontiff of burlesque pulpiteers' was a stirrer-up of fanatical hatred of Laudians and Catholics. He had named Charles 'Barabbas,' and before Naseby had ridden among the men with a Bible in one hand

[1] The identities of the executioner and his assistant have never been certainly solved. As this is a narrative, I have assumed my solution is correct. My reasons are given at some length in the section on this historical mystery in *Enigmas of History*: but they are too long, as the subject is too complicated, to be entered into here.

and a pistol in the other, urging them to do their duty and explaining that the sword contained all the laws of England. His shorter official exhortations were appreciated almost as greatly as his two-hour sermons. An example of them—on the text "Bind your Kings in chains and your nobles in fetters of iron"—was: "Beloved, this is the last psalm but one, and the next psalm hath six verses and twelve Halleujahs—praise ye the Lord. And for what? Look into my text! There you have the reason for it. Because the Kings were bound in chains."

Peters had come to hate the King with all the sadistic envy of his nature, and lost no opportunity to insult him personally. When Charles was being brought from Windsor to London for his trial, Peters ostentatiously rode in a coach just in front of him with his hat on and when a bystander dared to uncover to Charles, Peters ordered his troopers to throw him into the ditch, 'horse and all.' He installed himself in St. James's and encouraged the guard to commit those insults—including watching Charles while he relieved nature—which Tomlinson had eventually stopped. But not even Tomlinson could prevent Peters preaching in the palace chapel so that the King, had he wished to worship there, would have had to endure his tirades.

His sermon on the first Sunday of the King's trial was prefaced with "I have prayed and preached these twenty years and now I may say with old Simeon, Lord, now lettest thou thy servant depart in peace, for mine eyes have seen thy salvation" and added, in his characteristic *faux bonhomme* manner: "But soft there! I must not talk so here. I am in the King's chapel." On the Sunday after sentence was pronounced—last Sunday, two days ago—he had preached before Cromwell and others from the text: "All the kings of the nations, even all of them, lie in glory, every one in his own house. But thou art cast out of thy grave like an abominable branch, and as the raiment of those that are slain, thrust through with a sword, that go down to the stones of the pit as a carcass trodden under foot." "This," remarked Peters, "I did intend to insist and preach upon before the poor wretch, but the poor wretch would not hear me."

It was not, however, because of Charles's known aversion to Peters that he had not been selected to-day as one of the five godly ministers to purvey spiritual comfort. It was because there was other and more important work for Peters to do and when he met Nunnelly he was on his way to superintend one part of it.

In the Banqueting Hall, they met Francis Tench, once the King's pulley-maker, who had been ordered to wait there for Peters. Tench shared Peters's personal hatred of the King, but for a more comprehensible reason. Four years earlier, Charles had hanged his brother at Oxford for spying. Thereupon Tench had left the Royal service and set up on his own as an ironmonger and joiner at the Sign of the Drum in Houndsditch. He had made himself prominent at the King's trial among the spectators by his vociferous cries for 'Justice! Justice!' and had offered his service to Blackwell, the Overseer of Works, in the construction of the scaffold for the last stage of the 'glorious work.'

Peters had suggested that, in case Charles struggled, ropes and pulleys should be provided to drag him to the block 'like a beast.' The idea had been greeted with enthusiasm. One of the workmen, Lockier had been dispatched to fetch four iron staples from the nearest ironmonger in King Street and now Tench, as an expert, had been summoned to fix the pulleys.

Peters immediately greeted Tench, and gave him orders in a low voice that Nunnelly could not hear. The purport of them was plain enough, however, for Tench immediately went out on to the scaffold and superintended the fixing of the staples to which his ropes and pulleys would be attached.

"What are you doing?" Nunnelly asked when he came back to the Hall. "Are you turning hangman?"

"This will be a happy day for me," Tench replied.

"Pray God send it be not a bloody day for us all," retorted Nunnelly.

Before they could say more, Peters returned from inspecting Tench's work on the scaffold and he and Tench hurried back to St. James's.

Peters, who had procured for himself the best apartments in St. James's, wanted to establish an alibi. He did not think it would be difficult, as he had only kept with him as a servant Cornelius Glover, a raw youth just up from the country who wanted nothing better than to be out among the crowds on such an exciting day in such an exciting city. Peters intended to tell Cornelius that he felt ill—'melancholy sick'—and would keep his room all day, but that he would not on that account spoil his servant's pleasure. Cornelius could go out to watch the proceedings. And as soon as the youth had gone, leaving him in bed, Peters would steal back, quietly and unobtrusively, to Whitehall.

Tench on the other hand intended to go back to Whitehall, accompanying the King in the most public way possible.

Morning Service

At St. James's, the King was at his prayers. After he had sent the message that he did not wish to be troubled by the godly ministers, he invited Herbert to remain in attendance while Juxon read Mattins and celebrated Holy Communion.

There was, for them all, an added significance in that the day was a Tuesday, for Tuesdays at Court had always been set aside for special Sermons and, if Charles were any distance away, he would ride hard to be present at the beginning of them.

The King's punctilious observance of religious practices had been one of the distinguishing marks of his reign. His Court was ruled by it. On days when he went hunting, 'his beloved sport,' his Chaplains were called for service before daybreak, for, as one of his courtiers observed, "he was punctual and regular in his devotions, so that he was never known to enter upon his recreations or sports, though never so early in the morning, before he had been at public prayers; and he was likewise very strict in observing the hours of his private devotions." To his Puritan guards, Charles's ordered piety had been a perpetual marvel and his obvious sincerity had taken something of the sting out of his criticism of their own more unpredictable forms of worship: "In devotions I love neither profane boldness nor pious nonsense. I am equally scandalized with all prayers that sound either imperiously or rudely or passionately as either wanting humility to God or charity to men. I confess I am better pleased with such Public Forms of Prayer as are fitted to the Church's and every Christian's daily and common necessities; because I am by them better assured what I may join my heart unto than I can be of any man's *extempore* sufficiency."

Above everything else in his captivity, Charles had resented being deprived of his Chaplains, as he was during the earlier part of his imprisonment, and he left it on record: "When Providence was pleased to deprive me of all other civil comforts and secular attendants, I thought the absence of them all might be best supplied by the attendance of some of my chaplains. If I had asked my revenues, my power of militia or anyone of my kingdoms, it had been no wonder to be denied in those things; but to deny me the ghostly comfort of my chaplains seems a greater rigour and barbarity than is ever used by Christians to the meanest prisoners and greatest malefactors whom though the justice of the law deprives of worldly comforts, yet the mercy of religion allows them the benefit of their clergy, as not aiming at once to destroy their bodies and to damn their souls. I have sometimes thought the unChristianness of those denials might arise from a displeasure some men had to see me prefer my own divines before their ministers whom, though I respect for that worth and piety that may be in them, yet I cannot think proper for my present comforters or physicians who have (some of them at least) had so great an influence in occasioning these calamities and inflicting these wounds on me."[1]

Charles was not one of those who, on the point of death, return to a practice of religion which they have omitted for most of their life; for him there was in this respect no difference between this day and any other. What he did now, he had done publicly (as far as he was allowed) for the twenty-four years of his reign and privately all his life. In the formal simplicity of the services of his Church, he had by such use come to find the perfect expression of the spiritual values by which he lived; and the forms themselves became things of strength. On the most agonizing day of his life—the day that Buckingham was murdered—a courtier had whispered the news to him while he was at Morning Prayer. He heard it without any change of countenance and continued on his knees till the service was at an end. Not till the Blessing had been given did he retire to his room to throw himself on his bed in a passion of tears. And now that he himself was to die, the decorous liturgy would conduct him, fearless, to Christ.

Easter was early that year. It fell on Lady Day (and, by many, the proverbial warning

> Let the land beware of great mishap
> When Our Lord falls into Our Lady's lap

[1] There can be no doubt that the *Eikon Basilike* here expresses the King's mind perfectly, even if the phraseology owes something to an editor—and that is by no means 'proved.'

was considered to be spectacularly justified). Already Sexagesima was past and as Juxon read the proper collect, its appropriateness was inescapable: "O Lord God, who seest that we put not our trust in any thing that we do, mercifully grant that by thy power we may be defended against all adversity." The First Lesson, telling of the turning of the rivers of Egypt to blood because of Pharaoh's refusal to obey Moses and Aaron, the Lord's anointed, was unmistakably apposite. But it was the Second Lesson, which was St. Matthew's account of the trial and death of Christ, that most held the attention of them all. When the service was over and Mattins had been followed by Holy Communion, Charles asked Juxon whether he had chosen it purposely.

"No, sir," said Juxon, "it is the lesson appointed for to-day in the Kalendar."

Charles, strengthened by the aftermath of Gethsemane, said: "I am ready. Now let the rogues come when they will."

Across the Park

A minute or two before ten o'clock, there was a gentle knock at the door, just as there had been in Herbert's dream and, as in his dream, Herbert took no notice of it. It was followed by a second knock, this time louder and more peremptory, which Herbert still affected to disregard till Charles, who guessed its meaning, ordered him to open the door. Colonel Hacker stood there, looking considerably less self-possessed than usual.

"What do you want?" asked Herbert.

"I wish to speak to the King," said Hacker.

Charles called out: "Let him come in" and the Colonel advanced into the inner room to say that it was time to go to Whitehall where there would be further opportunity for the King to rest. Herbert noticed that Hacker was trembling, but ascribed it to the wrong cause. He could not know, as Hacker knew only too well, the difficulties which were making the great public act of justice take on more and more the complexion of a private plot whose success was even now hanging in the balance. It was fear for the Cause, not any sudden shudder of embarrassment at leading his King to death, that was affecting the Colonel. Francis Hacker—the only renegade in a landed Nottinghamshire family of Royalists—had a fanatical devotion to the principles he had espoused. Throughout the wars, he had fought with a tenacity which, when he was on two occasions taken prisoner, had made him scorn a pardon. He gave 'all the prizes he ever took' to the party and to his soldiers. Of all men, he was the least likely to weaken now.

"Go outside and wait for me," said the King. "I will be with you in a moment."

Hacker withdrew and, at a sign from Charles, Juxon, Herbert and Tomlinson also went into the outer room, leaving the King for the first and last time that day completely alone.

When, after a short interval, Charles joined them, he was entirely master of himself and, taking Juxon by the hand and smiling, said: "Come, let us be going." He told Herbert to bring with him the little silver clock that hung by his bedside. To Hacker he merely remarked that, on such a cold morning, he was grateful for the walk as it would restore his circulation. Those of his old servants and acquaintances who were among the crowd outside noticed that his countenance was 'as cheerful as if he were going hunting, a pastime he was much pleased with.'

As they passed from the palace garden into the walled Park, there was a deafening roll of drums, intended to drown any manifestation of popular sympathy. The King stopped and asked Herbert the time and when Herbert, looking at the bedside clock, told him, he took the clock into his own hand and presented it, as it were officially, to the faithful servant, asking him keep it as a memorial.

The companies of infantry were drawn up in double lines on each side of the path running across the Park from the garden-entrance of St. James's to the nearest part of Whitehall—the steps leading from a door in the Park wall to the gallery over the upper part of the Holbein Gate.[1] Behind the soldiers, spectators, some in sympathy, some in hatred, most in curiosity, watched the procession.

At the head marched the company of halberdiers commanded by Hacker, with drums beating and banners flying. Then came the King, with Juxon on his right and Colonel Tomlinson, bareheaded, on his left. Herbert walked a little behind followed by the King's guards commanded by Tomlinson's deputies, Lieutenant-Colonel Ralph Cobbett and Captain John Merriman. More halberdiers brought up the rear.

So slow was the pace of the march, matching the solemnity of the occasion, that the King, who was a very fast walker, asked them to quicken their step. To those in front of him he called out 'March apace.' The soldiers obeyed this last command. To Juxon he remarked, "I am going to a heavenly crown with less solicitude than I have often encouraged men to fight for my earthly one" and then turned to speak to Tomlinson.

During the night, he told him, he had been thinking of their earlier conversation about his burial. It had occurred to him that Prince Charles might, after all, decide to come over from France to bury him. Whether he envisaged a sudden restoration of the monarchy as part of the nation's revulsion of feeling after his own death or whether he thought Charles might ask for a safe-conduct to perform a natural act of filial piety, he did not say. He was concerned only to ensure that, should the new King come, he should not

[1] Approximately where Dover House now stands.

be hurt by finding that his father had not allowed for the possibility and that the funeral arrangements had been officially carried out by Richmond.

"You will see to it that I am not buried immediately—not before my son Charles has had time to come?"

"I will do all that is in my power, sir," said Tomlinson, "and I promise that I will communicate your desire to the Duke of Richmond and to the Lord General Fairfax."

Charles thanked him and Tomlinson, slowly and with considerable embarrassment, asked if he might be permitted to put a question to the King. Now, at this last moment, there was one thing that the Colonel felt he had to know. He had been a boy of eight when King James had died and Charles had become King. Brought up in Puritan surroundings, he had imbibed in those young impressionable years, all the fierce anti-Royalist propaganda of the times. In his twenties, his certainty of the King's wickedness had made him take up arms against 'the man of blood.' Until five weeks ago, he had still believed it, but the more he had seen of Charles, the more impossible he had found it to connect the real man with the vile stories, especially with the chief article of the Puritan myth, that Charles was, in the strict sense of the term, a murderer, in that he was an accessory of the Duke of Buckingham in his poisoning of King James.[1] John Milton himself, brushing aside technicalities, had reduced the matter to its simplest terms: "To omit other evidences, he that would not suffer a Duke that was accused of it to come to his trial must needs have been guilty of it himself."

"What is your question?" said the King.

"Is it true, sir," Tomlinson asked, "that you concurred

[1] I have expressed the matter in this way because it seems to me that, considering all the evidence, there can be no reasonable doubt that Buckingham did poison James (though, equally certainly, Charles had no knowledge of it). The subject is too complicated to discuss here and readers are referred to my *Enigmas of History* for an analysis of it.

with the Duke of Buckingham in causing your father's death?"

"My friend," said Charles, "if I had no other sin than that, as God knows, I should have no need to beg His forgiveness at this hour." His gentle, incredulous smile gave Tomlinson pardon before he asked it.

Quickly, with his perfect tact, Charles changed the subject. They were passing the entrance to the Spring Garden. Charles pointed towards it.

It had been in Spring Garden, more than anywhere else, that in the happy mid-thirties, Charles had been accustomed to rub shoulders with his subjects. The Garden stood at the north-east corner of St. James's Park, a stone's throw from Charing Cross.[1] Its name was taken from a spring or fountain which sprinkled anyone who came to consult the sundial and happened to tread on the hidden machinery. But it was not this Elizabethan eccentricity which accounted for the Garden's popularity; or even its formal groves or its view of St. James's Park or its abundance in summer of such plants as sweet-briar and honeysuckle, jessamine and musk-rose, lavender and rosemary (chosen because their fragrance made them 'aptest to tinge the air upon every gentle emission at a great distance'). Its less formal thickets 'contrived to all the advantages of gallantry' were an attraction more potent than such simple delights.

Charles, in search of revenue, had allowed a public bowling-green to be licensed there—which had meant high wagers and heavy drinking. He had himself lost as much as £1,000 on a single game of bowls, though the usual stakes were the more modest £10 a game; and the losers were apt to become quarrelsome. There was no stint of refreshment, for a licence had also been granted for 'an ordinary of six

[1] The corner where it joins St. James's Park and where 'Henry's tree' stood is still commemorated in the name 'Spring Garden' near the present Admiralty Arch.

shillings a meal' which consisted of 'certain trifling tarts, neats' tongues, salacious meats and bad Rhenish.' Among other attractions there were butts and a pheasant yard.

However satisfactory from the point of view of revenue public admission had been, the tone of Spring Garden had soon deteriorated to the point of embarrassment. Strafford, in Ireland, was told by a correspondent that it had become "scandalous and insufferable; continual bibbing and drinking wine all day under the trees; two or three quarrels every week," and Charles had had to take action about it. Young George Digby and Will Crofts had had a violent quarrel there and when Digby was reprimanded for striking Crofts in the King's Garden he had insolently retorted that 'he took it for a common bowling-place where all paid money for their coming in.' The Garden was thereupon closed to the public, but Queen Henrietta—Crofts was her Captain of the Guard—interceded for it and it was temporarily reprieved, on condition there was no more bowling.

The Garden was closed now, for it had no place in a Puritan London; and the deadness of this winter day emphasized its forlornness. Looking at it for the last time, Charles noticed only the bare tree standing at the corner where the Garden joined the Park. The tree was almost his own age.

"You see that tree," he said to Tomlinson. "My brother Henry planted it."

The procession, leaving Henry's tree, skirted the lake and the piece of water known as Rosamond's Pond, and marched towards the gate that led to Whitehall. Abreast of the King, running every now and then a little ahead of him so that he might stare closely at him in an attempt to embarrass him was Francis Tench. He had waited in St. James's till the procession started and was able, as a privileged person, to accompany it closely. He had also, unexpectedly, another advantage. The King's favourite spaniel, Rogue, though he should have been in the kennels with the other dogs waiting to be sent to the Queen, had managed to elude the guards and had scampered after his master for a walk in the Park. But he did not manage to elude Tench, who, making a dive at him, caught him and kept him firmly in his arms.[1]

Tench was now devoting all his energies in endeavouring to break Charles's nerve. As long as the King had been talking to Tomlinson, he had not noticed him; but now, as he turned to speak to Juxon, on the other side of him, he found Tench's relentless stare inescapable. "The Bishop of London, though not easily angered, was much offended hereat, as done out of despiteful design, to discompose him before his death and moved the Captain of the Guard to take him away." Hacker sent Tench about his business.

They had now arrived at the outside staircase leading over the Holbein Gate. Charles ran quickly up the steps and so into his Palace of Whitehall.

The Scene of the Crime

The Holbein Gate straddled across the road, large and arrogant like the King who had had it built. Henry VIII had wanted a gallery by which he could pass easily from Whitehall to the Tennis Court, the Cockpit and the Bowling Green which were part of the Park on the other side of the road. From the gallery, too, he could also watch sports in the Tilt-Yard or the other displays that, on special occasions, took place in the Park.

Standing at right-angles to the Banqueting House—indeed, almost touching it at the Westminster end—the Holbein Gate had now an old-fashioned appearance. Its century-old Tudor style, with battlements and towers, formed a striking contrast to the neo-Classic simplicity of Inigo Jones's new building. The Gate's dull red brickwork

[1] After the execution, Tench put Rogue and the pulleys he provided for the scaffold on exhibition.

in diaper pattern looked dark against the Banqueting House's whiteness and the ornamental busts of Henry VIII, his father and other Tudor worthies which decorated it and had once been bright with paint, were now revealing the terra-cotta beneath.

From the upper windows of the Gate, as Charles passed through the gallery, he could have seen spread at his feet the little part of London where he was to play his tragedy to its conclusion. To the north was the stump of Charing Cross[1] and beyond it in the fields his own parish church of St. Martin. The Cross itself, that lovely memorial of a king to his dead queen, with its painted and gilded figures of saints, had been broken up and pulled down in a Puritan fury of iconoclasm eighteen months earlier and the Caen stone and the Dorset marble of it used for making knife-hafts. The stump was still there as a landmark, but that too was in process of demolition and the ballad-makers ironically lamented the end of a landmark:

> Undone, undone the lawyers are—
> They wander about the town,
> Nor can find the way to Westminster,
> Now Charing Cross is down.
> At the end of the Strand they make a stand,
> Swearing they are at a loss,
> And chaffing say, That's not the way
> They must go by Charing Cross.

That morning there was no doubt about the way. All London seemed to have swarmed along the Strand and down into the long rectangle stretching between the buildings from the Holbein Gate to the mutilated Cross. At each extremity, a troop of picked cavalry was stationed and round the scaffold itself lines of soldiers were drawn up to keep the populace at their proper distance.

[1] On the place where his own statue now stands.

So, from the windows of the Holbein Gate, Charles could have seen them making the street a sea of heads, while at the guardroom (which stood opposite the Banqueting House) and, on the roof as well as at the windows of Wallingford House beyond it, where Buckingham had once lived, spectators were crowding.

On the Westminster side of the Holbein Gate, the length of the Privy Garden away from it, was the other, less magnificent, Gatehouse, known as the King's Gate. This formed the north boundary of King Street, which led to Westminster Hall and Westminster Abbey, two minutes' walk away. King Street was one of the most thickly populated districts of the capital whose inhabitants, in normal times, did a thriving trade in letting lodgings to Members of Parliament and other gentlemen visiting London. But recently it had fallen on bad times and the two-hundred-or-so new houses which had been hastily and illegally erected to catch the boom of ten years ago were falling into a squalor and dilapidation which matched the older tenements. The turnings off King Street—Thieving Lane and Antelope Alley and Cherry Tree Court and the rest—were breeding grounds for vice and disease; and the meanness of these slums was accentuated by the magnificence of the Hall and the Abbey within a stone's throw of them. But this morning they were all deserted and their inhabitants had made their way to the other side of King's Gate and the Holbein Gate, from which point alone they could watch the scaffold.

The King's Gate, as Charles saw it for the last time from the southern windows of the Holbein Gate, held for him one inescapable memory; for it was from there, in a room over the arch of the Gate, that his wife had watched his coronation procession going from Westminster Hall to the Abbey. It wanted but three days to the anniversary of his crowning twenty-three years ago under just such leaden, cold skies—and that day was finding now its complement and fulfilment in this. February 2, 1626, was as unique among coronations of the Kings of England as to-day, January 30, 1649, was to be among their deaths. And that the one was connected with the other was held as an article of superstitious faith by a mass of people whose religious and political loyalties and explanations of the present killing were, by comparison, superficial.

That Henrietta Maria, as a Catholic, had refused to be crowned at a Protestant service and had even refused to witness her husband's crowning from behind the lattice which had been prepared for her in the Abbey, was only one of the misfortunes of the day. Because it was Candlemas Day, Charles had insisted on wearing white instead of the traditional purple, ignoring the prophecy attributed to Merlin that white possessed the most unhappy import for the throne of England and that a 'White King' was a figure of doom.

Not only the King's personal attire but part of the official regalia itself was found wanting. The sceptre with the dove, the emblem of peace, was found just before the Coronation to have been damaged. The left wing of the dove had been broken. Charles had instructed his goldsmith that the break was to be made good without any mark remaining visible. The goldsmith answered that such a thing was impossible. "Then if you cannot do it," said the King angrily, "another shall." Accordingly the goldsmith, anxious not to lose his appointment had substituted an entirely new dove—a piece of vandalism to a relic of King Edward the Confessor which was only discovered subsequently.

The King had been anointed by the Archbishop of Canterbury, George Abbot, who had been suspended from his episcopal functions because four years earlier he had accidentally killed a game-keeper. At the time, King James had remarked that "no one but a fool or a knave would think the worse of him; it might be any man's case" but, as by Canon Law, he had committed, however unwittingly, an irregularity, he was suspended and neither John Williams nor William Laud (who, the year of the accident, were given their first bishoprics) would consent to be consecrated 'by a man whose hands were dipped in blood.' Yet, strangely, he had been allowed to pour the oil of unction on the new King's head at his hallowing,[1] to the scandal of many simple souls.

Nor was this the last of the evil omens. Preparations had been made to receive the King, who came by the Royal Barge the little way from Whitehall to Westminster, at Sir Robert Cotton's Stairs. By mischance, the Barge missed these steps on which the carpets had been laid in readiness and ran aground in the mud at the bottom of the Parliament stairs, with the result that Charles and his attendants had had to land with what dignity they could muster, assisted by certain neighbouring boats.

Worse still, at the first ceremony which took place after Charles had entered the Abbey—the Recognition—there had been a strange mischance. When a new King comes to his crowning, the Primate addresses the assembled congregation, presenting the sovereign, who stands before his Chair of State, and demanding an acclamation of fealty. An eyewitness in the Abbey at Charles's coronation, Sir Symonds d'Ewes (who was, at the moment, one of the Members of Parliament excluded from Parliament) had thus described the scene: "His Majesty presenting himself bare-headed to the people, the Archbishop on his right hand and the Earl Marshall on his left, the Archbishop said in my articulate hearing: 'My masters and friends, I am here come to present unto you your king, King Charles, to whom the crown of his ancestors and predecessors is now devolved by

[1] As Canon Jocelyn Perkins has written in *The Hallowing of the Sovereigns of England*: "The whole thing seems quite unintelligible. It may fairly be described as having been one of the 'mysteries' which are furnished by the history of our English coronations."

lineal right, and he himself come hither to be settled in that throne which God and his birth have appointed for him; and therefore I desire you by your general acclamation to testify your consent and willingness thereto.' Upon which, whether some expected that he should have spoken more; or that others, not hearing well what he said hindered those, by questioning, which might have heard; or that the newness and greatness of the action busied men's thoughts; or that the presence of so dear a king drew an admiring silence; or that those who were nearest doubted what to do: but *not one word followed* till my Lord of Arundel told them they should cry out, 'God save King Charles.' Upon which, as if ashamed of their first oversight, a little shouting followed."

But if men were still, Nature was not. During the actual ceremony there had been the shock of an earthquake of such violence that all persons in the immediate neighbourhood of the Abbey had been terrified out of their senses.

And last, but now most potently in the King's memory, had been the text which the preacher, Dr. Senhouse, had chosen for the sermon, a text generally considered to have been fitter for a funeral than for a coronation. But over the years, echoing from the ritual of that day to the ritual of this, the words "Be thou faithful unto death and I will give thee a crown of life" had gained new potency as the King entered Whitehall to fulfil his destiny and to exchange his crown.

The Palace of Whitehall

The Palace of Whitehall resembled a magnificent untidy village. Its twenty-three acres, stretching east and west from the Thames to St. James's Park; and north and south, from Wallingford House to King's Gate,[1] housed, not only the Royal apartments, the Chapel, the Great Hall and the Banqueting House, but also the houses, apartments and

[1] i.e. from the Admiralty to Downing Street.

other buildings where the host of courtiers and servants, officials and servants' servants lived and worked. There were the kitchens and cellars and pantries and spiceries; the cyder-house and the wine-cellar and the brew-house for small-beer; the bakehouses and the slaughter-houses; the wash-yards and the coal-yards. For the custom had persisted since the days of Henry VIII who had rebuilt the Palace a century ago that everything that could be made in the Palace should be made there and stored under responsible officers.

When Charles had been in residence there the bountiful supply of food at his tables was a subject of amazement for foreigners. The King's table had twenty-eight dishes and the Queen's, twenty-four. There were four other tables, each provided with sixteen dishes; three with ten; twelve with seven; seventeen with five; thirty with four; thirty-two with three and thirteen with two. In all, there had been about five hundred dishes at each meal for the visitors and the inhabitants of Whitehall in their due gradations.

The sprawling Palace gave the impression of having grown, as a village might grow, except in the newer part which Henry VIII had planned after a devastating fire had destroyed much of the old building. Now the rabbit-warren of little streets and narrow passages and alleys surrounded and intersected the three Courts, which gave it what design it possessed.

A French visitor of the time recorded: "Whitehall consists of a Great Court surrounded by buildings without either symmetry or beauty worth mentioning, having a Chapel which occupies the entire face of that Court and looks towards the gate through which one enters, where on the right hand there is a great pavilion with many windows, which seems newly built and fronts the place before the river." (This, of course, was the Banqueting House.)

The second Court, the rectangle through which the visitor first entered, led northwards to the third Court, Scotland

Yard (which stood in the site of the palace 'for the receipt of the Kings of Scotland when they came to the Parliament of England'), which now contained the Guard House.

To the south of the three Courts—and beyond the south end of the Banqueting House—was the Privy Garden which alone met with the French observer's approval: "On the side looking toward the river there is a garden in which there is a parterre, many statues of marble and bronze, well executed, and a terrace by the side of the river." Here in the garden was the great sundial which King James had had made as a present for Charles, twenty-five years ago by Edward Gunter, the Professor of Astronomy at Gresham College. On the great square block of stone, nearly four feet high and weighing five tons, Gunter had made nine sundials. The top bore one at each corner and 'a fifth in the middle which was the chief of all, the great horizontal concave'; and there were east, west, north and south dials at the sides.

It was to the magnificent Cabinet-Chamber and its connected apartments, including the so-called Horn-Chamber, overlooking the Privy Garden that Charles was now taken. Passing to it along the great Gallery, he was once more among the masterpieces of art which he had spent his reign in collecting and for which he deserved the title of the Connoisseur of Europe—or, as Rubens had expressed it, "le prince le plus amateur de la peinture qui sout au monde." Parliament had not yet carried out to the full the ordinance they had made four years earlier that "all such pictures and statues as are without any superstition shall be sold for the benefit of Ireland" (that is to say, the war in Ireland) while "all such pictures as have the representation of the Second Person of the Trinity and all such pictures as have the representation of the Virgin Mary shall be forthwith burnt." Even the later and more sweeping proposals to sell all the works of art and apply the first thirty thousand pounds to the needs of the navy had not been implemented.

And in the Gallery and the Cabinet-Chamber, where Charles had concentrated the major masterpieces of that unrivalled collection which would be dispersed on his death, he could be comforted by that beauty whose quest had been half his life.

The iconoclasts, even in their fanaticism of hatred for Christ's Mother, had spared Raphael's *Holy Family* and Caravaggio's *Death of the Virgin*, del Sarto's *Assunto mistico* and Veronese's *Marriage at Cana*. There were still scenes from the earthly life of the Second Person of the Trinity—Tintoretto's *Christ washing the feet of the Disciples* and van Haarlem's *Descent from the Cross*, Titian's *Supper at Emmaus* and Mantegna's *Christ carrying the Cross*.

The secular pictures such as Mantegna's unsurpassed *Triumph of Julius Caesar* were safe enough and the portraits, ancient and modern—Gorgione's self-portrait and Titian's Charles V and even Tintoretto's Ignatius Loyola (which had mercifully been unrecognized) and Holbein's Thomas More (which had been surprisingly left unscathed); and the familiar family faces, Clouet's portrait of Mary Queen of Scots and Van Dyck's many paintings of Charles's wife and children and a Rubens portrait of Buckingham.

In the quiet of the Cabinet-Chamber, where the noise of the streets came but faintly across the Privy Garden, Charles was left with Herbert and Juxon, while Tomlinson went outside to glean what information he could.

Son to Father

As Tomlinson went through the outer room the guards on duty told him that there was a visitor who was persistently trying to get access to the King. They would not, of course, allow it. He was outside walking up and down the Gallery.

When the Colonel went out to him and asked him his business he discovered that the man was Henry Seymour, who had once been Page of Honour to the King, but who at the outbreak of war had been attached to the Prince of Wales and had gone with him to France. The younger Charles was now using him as his envoy and had sent him to England bearing the blank sheet of paper with the Prince's signature attached on which Fairfax, in the name of the Army, might write what terms he chose for the King's life. Seymour had also a personal letter from Prince Charles to his father which he wished to deliver in person. Could the Colonel allow it? And, if not, would the Colonel give it to the King?

Without hesitation, Tomlinson took Seymour straight through to Charles. He could not, as Seymour understood, leave them alone, but he would exercise the discreetest of surveillances during their conversation. He could talk to Herbert in a corner of the room while Seymour delivered the Prince's messages and listened to the King's replies.

The unexpected kindness of Tomlinson, combined with the altered appearance of the King whom Seymour had not seen for five years—grey, thin, with the aura of death already round him—suddenly broke the envoy's nerve. As soon as he entered the room, he fell on his knees and burst into a flood of tears. Herbert, who was finding his own self-control lessening every minute, noted: "Mr. Seymour, at his entrance, fell into a passion, having formerly seen His Majesty in a glorious state, and now in a dolorous; and having kissed the King's hand, clasped about his legs lamentably mourning. Hacker came in and was abashed."

Hacker, however, did not stay. It was not yet his hour of command, and until he came to conduct the King to the scaffold, the responsibility for Charles's person was still Tomlinson's. Also Hacker had his own worries at that moment.

Seymour gradually recovered himself, helped by Charles's own iron self-control, and handed the King his son's letter.

"Sir," it ran, "having no means to come to the knowledge of Your Majesty's present condition but such as I receive from the prints or (what is uncertain) report, I have sent this bearer, Seymour, to wait upon Your Majesty and to bring me an account of it; that I may withal assure Your Majesty I do not only pray for Your Majesty according to my duty; but shall always be ready to do all which shall be in my power to deserve that blessing which I now humbly beg of Your Majesty upon, Sir, Your Majesty's most humble and most obedient son and servant, Charles."

The note, so careful in its formality of phrase (lest it should fall into other and dangerous hands), was dated from the Hague six days earlier—January 23. But with it, reckless of danger, the Prince had enclosed that which would assure his father of his affection—another blank sheet with his signature affixed. When Seymour explained that he had already delivered one to Fairfax and that the Prince was content to forego everything, even the succession, in return for his father's life, Charles smiled and answered the gesture of love by another. He threw the blank paper into the fire.

Then, having heard all the news from abroad, he gave Seymour his last messages for the Prince. He had written them in that long, careful letter which he had entrusted to Herbert to deliver when there should be opportunity. If Seymour took it now, there was the possibility that it might be confiscated before he left Whitehall. Tomlinson's writ did not run further than the room and the guards at the gates were not likely to waive a search. It might be better if he called on Herbert when to-day's business was over and took it from him then. Meanwhile Seymour could remember the tenor of it, and the other messages to the Prince, and his love and dying blessing.

Father to Son

The letter which the King had written to the Prince ran:

Son, if these papers with some others, wherein I have set down the private reflections of my conscience, and my most impartial thoughts, touching the chief passages which have been most remarkable, or disputed in my late troubles, come to your hands, to whom they are chiefly designed; they may be so far useful to you, as to state your judgment aright in what hath passed: whereof a pious is the best use that can be made; and they may also give you some directions, how to remedy the present distempers, and prevent (if God will) the like for time to come.

It is some kind of deceiving and lessening the injury of my long restraint, when I find my leisure and solitude have produced something worthy of myself, and useful to you, that neither you, nor any other, may hereafter measure my cause by the success; nor my judgments of things by my misfortunes; which I count the greater by far, because they have so far lighted upon you, and some others, whom I have most cause to love as well as myself; and of whose unmerited sufferings I have a greater sense than of my own.

But this advantage of wisdom you have above most princes; that you have begun, and now spent some years of discretion, in the experience of troubles, and exercise of patience, wherein piety, and all vertues both moral and political, are commonly better planted to a thriving, as trees set in winter, than in warmth and serenity of times; or amidst those delights, which usually attend princes courts in times of peace and plenty; which are prone, either to root up all plants of true vertue and honour; or to be contented only with some leaves and withering formalities of them, without any real fruits, such as tend to the public good, for which princes should always remember they are born, and by providence designed.

The evidence of which different education the Holy Writ affords us in the contemplation of David and Rehoboam: the one prepared by many afflictions for a flourishing kingdom; the other softened by the unparallelled prosperity of Solomon's Court; and so corrupted to the great diminution, both for Peace, Honour, and Kingdom, by those flatteries, which are as unseperable from prosperous princes, as flies are from fruit in summer; whom adversity, like cold weather, drives away.

I had rather you should be Charles le Bon, than le Grand, good, than great; I hope God hath designed you to be both; having so early put you into that exercise of his Graces and gifts bestowed upon you, which may best weed out all vitious inclinations, and dispose you to those princely indowments, and employments, which will most gain the love, and intend the welfare of those, over whom God shall place you. With God I would have you begin and end, who is King of Kings; the sovereign disposer of the Kingdoms of the World, who pulleth down one and setteth up another.

The best government, and highest sovereignty you can attain to, is, to be subject to him; that the Scepter of his word and Spirit may rule in your heart.

The true glory of Princes consists in advancing God's glory, in the maintenance of true religion, and the Churches good; also in the dispensation of civil power, with Justice and honour to the public peace.

Piety will make you prosperous; at least it will keep you from being miserable; nor is he much a loser, that loseth all, yet saveth his own soul at last.

To which center of true happiness God (I trust) hath, and will graciously direct all these black lines of affliction, which he hath been pleased to draw on me, and by which he hath (I hope) drawn me nearer to himself. You have already tasted of that cup whereof I have liberally drunk; which I look upon as God's physick, having that in healthfulness which it wants in pleasure.

Above all I would have you, as I hope you are already, well-grounded and settled in your religion: the best profession of which I have ever esteemed that of the Church of England, in which you have been educated; yet I would have your own judgment and reason now seal to that sacred bond which education hath written; that it may be judiciously your own religion, and not other mens custom or tradition which you profess.

In this I charge you to persevere, as coming nearest to God's word for doctrine, and to the primitive examples for government, with some little amendment, which I have otherwise expressed, and often offered, though in vain. Your fixation in matters of religion will not be more necessary for your souls, than your kingdom's peace, when God shall bring you to them.

For I have observed, that the Devil of rebellion doth commonly turn himself into an angel of reformation; and the old serpent can pretend new light: when some mens consciences accuse them for sedition and faction, they stop its mouth with the name and noise of religion; when piety pleads for peace and patience, they cry out zeal.

So that, unless in this point you be well settled, you shall never want temptations to destroy you and yours, under pretension of reforming matters of religion, for that seems even to the worst of men, as the best and most auspicious beginning of their worst designs.

Where, besides the novelty which is taken enough with the vulgar, every one hath an affection, by seeming forward to an outward reformation of religion, to be thought zealous; hoping to cover those irreligious deformities, whereto they are conscious, by a severity of censuring other mens opinions and actions.

Take heed of abbetting any factions, or applying to any public discriminations in matters of religion, contrary to what is in your judgment, and the Churches well settled; your partial adhering as head to any one side, gains you not so great advantages in some mens hearts (who are prone to be of their king's religion) as it loseth you in others; who think themselves and their profession first despised, then persecuted by you: take such a course as may either with calmness and charity quite remove the seeming differences and offences by impartiality; or so order affairs in point of power that you shall not need to fear or flatter any faction.

For, if ever you stand in need of them, or must stand to their courtesy, you are undone: the serpent will devour the dove: you may never expect less of loyalty, justice, or humanity, than from those who engage into religious rebellion; their interest is always made God's; under the colours of piety, ambitious policies march, nor only with greatest security, but applause, as to the populacy; you may hear from them Jacob's voice, but you shall feel they have Esau's hands. Nothing seemed less considerable than the Presbyterian faction in England for many years, so compliant they were to public order; nor indeed was their party great either in Church or State, as to mens judgments; but as soon as discontents drave men into sidings, as ill humours fall to the disaffected part, which causes inflammations, so did all at first, who affected any novelties, adhere to that side, as the most remarkable and specious note of difference (then) in point of religion.

All the lesser factions at first were officious servants to Presbytery, their great master: till time and military success, discovering to each their peculiar advantages, invited them to part stakes: and leaving the joint stock of uniform religion, they pretended each to drive for their party the trade of profits and preferments to the breaking and undoing not only of the Church and State; but even of Presbytery itself, which seemed and hoped at first to have ingrossed all.

Let nothing seem little or despicable to you in matters which concern religion and the Churches peace, so as to neglect as speedy reforming and effectual suppressing errors and schisms: what seem at first but as a hand breadth, by seditious spirits, as by strong winds, are soon made to cover and darken the whole heaven.

When you have done justice to God, your own soul and his Church, in the profession and preservation both of truth and unity in religion; the main hinge upon which your prosperity will depend, and move, is that of civil justice, wherein the settled laws of these kingdoms, to which you are rightly heir, are the most excellent rules you can govern by, which by an admirable temperament give very much to subjects industry, liberty, and happiness: and yet reserve enough to the majesty and prerogative of any king, who owns his people as subjects, not as slaves; whose subjection, as it preserves their property, peace and safety, so it will never diminish your rights, nor their ingenious liberties: which consist in the enjoyment of the fruits of their industry, and the benefit of those laws to which themselves have consented.

Never charge your head with such a crown, as shall by its heaviness oppress the whole body, the weakness of whose parts cannot return anything of strength, honour, or safety to the head, but a necessary debilitation and ruin.

Your prerogative is best shewed and exercised in remitting, rather than exacting the rigor of the Laws; there being nothing worse than legal tyranny.

In these two points, the preservation of established religion and laws, I may (without vanity) turn the reproach of my sufferings, as to the world's censure, into the honour of a kind of martyrdom, as to the testimony of my own conscience; the troublers of my kingdoms, having nothing else to object against me but this, that I prefer religion and laws established before those alterations they propounded.

And so indeed I do, and ever shall, till I am convinced by better arguments, than what hitherto have been chiefly used against me, tumults, armies and prisons.

I cannot yet learn that lesson, nor I hope ever will you, that it is safe for a King to gratify any faction with the perturbation of the laws, in which is wrapt up the public interest and the good of the community.

How God will deal with me, as to the removal of these pressures and indignities, which his justice by the very unjust hands of some of my subjects, hath been pleased to lay upon me, I cannot tell; nor am I much solicitous what wrong I suffer from men, while I retain in my soul what I believe is right before God.

I have offered all for reformation and safety, that in reason, honour and conscience I can; reserving only what I cannot consent unto, without an irreparable injury to my own soul, the Church and my people; and you also as the next and undoubted heir of my kingdoms.

To which if the divine providence, to whom no difficulties are insuperable, shall in his due time, after my decease bring you, as I hope he will, my counsel and charge to you is, that you seriously consider the former real, or objected miscarriages, which might occasion my troubles, that you may avoid them.

Never repose so much upon any man's single counsel, fidelitie and discretion, in managing affairs of the first magnitude (that is, matters of religion and justice), as to create in yourself or others, a diffidence of your own judgment, which is likely to be always more constant and impartial to the interests of your crown and kingdom than any man's.

Next, beware of exasperating any factions by the crossness and asperity of some men's passions, humours, or private opinions employed by you, grounded only upon the differences in lesser matters, which are but the skirts and suburbs of religion.

Wherein a charitable connivance and Christian toleration often dissipates their strength, whom rougher opposition fortifies; and puts the despised and oppressed party into such combinations, as may most enable them to get a full revenge on those they count their persecutors who are commonly assisted by that vulgar commiseration, which attends all, that are said to suffer under the notion of religion.

Provided the difference amount not to an insolent opposition of laws and government, or religion established, as to the essentials of them: Such motions and minings are intolerable.

Always keep up solid piety, and those fundamental truths, which mend both hearts and lives of men with impartial favour and justice.

Take heed that outward circumstances and formalities of religion devour not all, or the best encouragments of learning, industry, and piety; but, with an equal eye, and impartial hand, distribute favours and rewards to all men, as you find them for their real goodness both in abilities and fidelity worthy and capable of them.

This will be sure to gain you the hearts of the best and the most too; who, though they be not good themselves, yet are glad to see the severer ways of virtue at any time sweetened by temporal rewards.

I have, you see, conflicted with different and opposite

factions; (for so I must needs call and count all those that act not in any conformity to the laws established in Church and State) no sooner have they by force subdued what they call their common enemie (that is, all those that adhered to the laws, and to me), and are secure from that fear, but they are divided to so high a rivalry, as sets them more at defiance against each other, than against their first antagonist.

Time will dissipate all factions, when once the rough horns of private mens covetous and ambitious designs shall discover themselves; which were at first wrapt up and hidden under the soft and hidden pretensions of religion, reformation and liberty; as the wolf is not less cruel, so he will be more justly hated, when he shall appear no better than a wolf under sheep's clothing.

But as for the seduced train of the vulgar, who in their simplicity follow those disguises, my charge and counsel to you is, that, as you need no palliations for any designs (as other men), so you study really to exceed (in true and constant demonstrations of goodness, piety, and vertue towards the people) even all those men, that make the greatest noise and ostentations of religion: so you shall neither fear any detection, (as they do, who have but the face and mask of goodness) nor shall you frustrate the just expectations of your people; who cannot in reason promise themselves so much good from any subjects novelties, as from the virtuous constancy of their king.

When these mountains of congealed factions shall by the sunshine of God's mercy, and the splendour of your virtues be thawed and dissipated; and the abused vulgar shall have learned, that none are greater oppressors of their estates, liberties, and consciences than those men, that entitle themselves the patrons and vindicators of them, only to usurp power over them; Let then no passion betray you to any study of revenge upon those, whose own sin and folly will sufficiently punish them in due time.

But as soon as the forked arrow of factions emulations is drawn out, use all princely arts and clemency to heal the wounds; that the smart of the cure may not equal the anguish of the hurt.

I have offered acts of Indemnity and Oblivion, to so great a latitude, as may include all, that can but suspect themselves to be any ways obnoxious to the laws; and which might serve to exclude all future jealousies and insecurities.

I would have you always propense to the same way; whenever it shall be desired and accepted, let it be granted, not only as an act of state policy and necessity, but of Christian charity and choice.

It is all I have now left me, a power to forgive those that have deprived me of all; and I thank God I have a heart to do it: and joy as much in this grace, which God hath given me, as in all my former enjoyments; for this is a greater argument of God's love to me, than any prosperity can be.

Be confident (as I am) that the most of all sides, who have done amiss, have done so, not out of malice, but misinformation, or misapprehension of things.

None will be more loyal and faithful to me and you, than those subjects, who sensible of their errors, and our injuries, will feel in their own souls most vehement motives to repentance; and earnest desires to make some reparations for their former defects.

As your quality sets you beyond any duel with any subject; so the nobleness of your mind must raise you above the meditating any revenge or executing your anger upon the many.

The more conscious you shall be to your own merits, upon your people; the more prone you will be to expect all love and loyalty from them; and to inflict no punishment upon them for former miscarriages; you will have more inward complacency in pardoning one, than in punishing a thousand.

This I write to you, not despairing of God's mercy, and my subjects affections towards you, both which I hope, you will study to deserve; yet we cannot merit of God but by his own mercy.

If God shall see fit to restore me, and you after me, to those enjoyments which the laws have assigned to us; and no subjects without a high degree of guilt and sin can devest us of; then may I have better opportunity when I shall be so happy to see you in peace, to let you more fully understand the things that belong to God's glory, your own honour, and the kingdom's peace.

But if you never see my face again, and God will have me buried in such a barbarous imprisonment and obscurity (which the perfecting some mens designs requires) wherein few hearts that love me are permitted to exchange a word, or a look with me, I do require and entreat you as your father and your king, that you never suffer your heart to receive the least check against, or disaffection from the true religion established in the Church of England.

I tell you I have tried it, and after much search, and many disputes, have concluded it to be the best in the world; not only in the Community as Christian, but as also in the special notion, as reformed; keeping the middle way between the pomp of superstitious tyranny, and the meanness of fantastick anarchy.

Not but that (the draught being excellent as to the main, both for doctrine and government in the Church of England) some lines, as in very good figures, may happily need some sweetening or polishing; which might here have easily been done by a safe and gentle hand, if some mens precipitancy had not violently demanded such rude alterations, as would have quite destroyed all the beauty and proportions of the whole.

The scandal of the late troubles, which some may object and urge to you against the Protestant religion established in England, is easily answered to them, or your own thoughts in this, that scarce any one who hath been a beginner, or an active prosecutor of this late war against the Church, the Laws, and me, either was, or is, a true lover, embracer, or practiser of the protestant religion, established in England, which neither gives such rules, nor ever before set such examples.

'Tis true, some heretofore had the boldness to present threatening petitions to their princes and Parliaments, which others of the same faction (but of worse spirits) have now put in execution: but let not counterfeit and disorderly zeal abate your value and esteem of true piety; both of them are to be known by their fruits; the sweetness of vine and figtree is not to be despised, though the brambles and thorns should pretend to bear figs and grapes, thereby to rule over the trees.

Nor would I have you to entertain any aversation, or dislike of Parliaments; which in their right constitution with freedom and honour will never injure or diminish your greatness, but will rather be as interchangings of love, loyalty, and confidence, between a Prince and his people.

Nor would the events of this black Parliament have been other than such (however much biassed by factions in the elections) if it had been preserved from the insolencies of popular dictates, and tumultuary impressions; the sad effects of which, will no doubt, make all Parliaments after this more cautious to preserve that freedom and honour, which belongs to such assemblies (when once they have fully shaken off this yoke of vulgar encroachment) since the public interest consists in the mutual and common good both of Prince and people.

Nothing can be more happy for all, than in fair, grave, and honourable ways, to contribute their counsels in common, enacting all things by public consent, without tyranny and or tumults. We must not starve ourselves, because some have surfeited of wholesome food.

And if neither I, nor you be ever restored to our right, but God, in his severest justice, will punish my subjects with continuance in their sin, and suffer them to be deluded with the prosperity of their wickedness; I hope God will give me and you, that grace which will teach and enable us, to want, as well as to wear a crown; which is not worth taking up, or enjoying upon sordid, dishonourable, and irreligious terms.

Keep you to true principles of piety, vertue and honour; you shall never want a kingdom.

A principal point of your honour will consist in your deferring all respect, love and protection to your mother, my wife, who hath many ways deserved well of me, and chiefly in this, that having been a means to bless me with so many hopeful children; (all which, with their mother, I recommend to your love and care) she hath been content with incomparable magnanimity and patience to suffer both for, and with me and you.

My prayer to Almighty God is (whatever becomes of me, who am, I thank God, wrapt up and fortified in my own innocency, and his Grace), that he would be pleased to make you an anchor, or harbour rather, to these tossed and weather-beaten kingdoms; a repairer by your wisdom, justice, piety, valour, of what the folly and wickedness of some men have so far ruined, as to leave nothing entire in Church or State; to the Crown, the Nobility, the Clergy, or the Commons, either as to laws, liberties, estates, order, honour, conscience, or lives.

When they have destroyed me (for I know not how far God may permit the malice and cruelty of my enemies to proceed, and such apprehensions some men's words and actions have already given me), as I doubt not but my blood will cry aloud for vengeance to heaven; so I beseech God not to pour out his wrath upon the generality of the people who have either deserted me, or engaged against me, through the artifice and hypocrisie of their leaders, whose inward horrour will be their first tormentor; nor will they escape exemplary judgments.

For those that loved me, I pray God they may have no miss of me, when I am gon; so much I wish and hope, that all good subjects may be satisfied with the blessings of your presence and vertues.

For those that repent of any defects of their duty towards me, as I freely forgive them in the word of a Christian King; so I believe you will find them truly jealous, to repay, with interest, that loyalty and love to you, which was due to me.

In sum, what good I intended, do you perform, when God shall give you power: much good I have offered, more I purposed to Church and State, if times had been capable of it.

The deception will soon vanish, and the vizards will fall off apace; This mask of Religion on the face of Rebellion (for so it now plainly appears since my restraint and cruel usage, that they fought not for me, as was pretended), will not long serve to hide some mens deformities.

Happy times, I hope, attend you, wherein your subjects (by their miseries) will have learned, That religion to their God, and loyalty to their King, cannot be parted, without both their sin and their infelicity.

I pray God bless you and establish your Kingdoms in righteousness, your soul in true religion, and your honour in the love of God and your people.

And if God will have disloyalty perfected by my destruction, let my memory ever, with my name, live in you; as of your father, that loves you, and once a King of three flourishing kingdoms; whom God thought fit to honour, not only with the scepter and government of them, but also with the suffering many indignities and an untimely death for them; while I studied to preserve the rights of the Church, the power of the Laws, the honour of my Crown, the privilege of Parliaments, the liberties of my people and my own conscience, which I thank God, is dearer to me, than a thousand kingdoms.

I know God can, I hope he will restore me to my rights; I cannot dispair either of his mercy, or my peoples love and pitty.

At worst I trust I shall but go before you, to a better kingdom, which God hath prepared for me, and me for it, through my saviour Jesus Christ, to whose mercy I commend you, and all mine. Farewell, till we meet, if not on earth, yet in heaven.

But now Charles knew that there would be no meeting on earth and that long before Seymour could leave London, he would be dead.

The Ministers call again

After Seymour had left him, Charles rested for a little in quiet by himself. There was no indication of how long it would be before the last knock on the door would summon him to the scaffold and he wished to be alone to collect his thoughts. But when the knock came, it was not Hacker. It was the five godly ministers, who, undeterred by the King's rebuff at St. James's had followed him to Whitehall and now once more offered their services.

Juxon with a certain asperity sent them away at once,

without any reference to the King. In spite of having the door shut in their face, they knocked again and this time insisted that the Bishop should deliver their message. It might be that the King would wish to see them and they were not, in any case, accustomed to taking orders from Bishops.

Charles, when he was told, merely asked Juxon to send them away.

"I have already told them that, Your Majesty," the Bishop explained, "but they will not be satisfied. They insist on an answer from you."

"Then," said Charles, "thank them from me for the tender of themselves; but tell them plainly that they, who have so often and causelessly prayed against me, shall never pray with me in this agony."

Juxon nodded approvingly and went back to the door to deliver the uncompromising message.

"But," Charles added, "tell them too that they may if they please—and I'll thank them for it—pray for me."

(II) AFTERNOON

The King breaks his fast

NOON struck and still death delayed. They prepared dinner for the King, but he refused to touch it. He had purposed that the last food and drink to pass his lips should be that Bread and Wine of the Holy Sacrament which were the Body and Blood of Christ. As he had been fasting when he received them, he had had nothing to eat all day.

Juxon remonstrated with him. Had he gone, as he had supposed he would, from the altar to the scaffold, his resolution would have been good and seemly. But things had fallen out otherwise. No one could tell how long he would have to wait. In this bitterly cold weather, he might faint upon the scaffold, unless he took a little nourishment. He would need his strength, too, for the speech to the people. However worthy the motive for abstinence, circumstances now made it imprudent. It was, indeed, his duty to take a little food and drink.

Charles, who had been accustomed all his life to eating 'heartily' and, while preferring plain food, to taking 'a good quantity thereof,' saw the force of the Bishop's argument. He was very hungry. He would eat a little, though nothing but bread and wine. He had half a 'manchet', a small bun-shaped loaf of white bread, and a glass of claret.

After he had finished, he fell to his prayers again.

The Warrant for the Headsman

In Ireton's apartments in Whitehall, he and Harrison, still suffering from the cold, were lying together in the bed, trying to keep warm, while Cromwell was explaining to

Colonel Francis Hacker, Lieutenant-Colonel Robert Phayre and Colonel Hercules Huncks that it devolved on them to sign the warrant for the executioner, once he had been found.

The details of the execution itself had been entrusted to them by the warrant issued by the Commissioners the previous day. "Whereas Charles Stuart, King of England, is and standeth convicted, attainted and condemned of High Treason and other high crimes; and sentence upon Saturday last was pronounced against him by this Court to be put to death by the severing of his head from his body, of which sentence execution yet remains to be done; These are therefore to will and require you to see the sentence executed in the open street before Whitehall upon the morrow, being the thirtieth day of this instant month of January between the hours of ten in the morning and five in the afternoon of the same day with full effect. And, for so doing, this shall be your sufficient warrant. And these are to require all officers and soldiers and other good people of this nation to be assisting unto you in this service. Given under our hands and seals."

This was the warrant which, lying on the table in the Painted Chamber, Cromwell had had difficulty in getting all the Commissioners to sign. But the fifty-nine signatures eventually procured (or, at least, entered there) were sufficient authority for the three to whom it was collectively and individually addressed. On Hacker, Huncks and Phayre, it now devolved, in virtue of this general warrant, to draw up and sign the particular warrant for the executioner.

There was, of course, no doubt about Hacker's co-operation; but Huncks and Phayre were less predictable. They had both been among the forty halberdiers attending the Court for the trial of the King, and Huncks had, three months earlier, been appointed Governor of Londonderry, which might have been interpreted as a gesture of

Cromwellian confidence. On the other hand both had been concerned with the Irish rather than with the English side of the war—Phayre was the son of the vicar of Kilshanning in Cork, and Huncks was now in England only temporarily, engaged in raising a regiment to take back for service in Ireland. Consequently neither was infected by the immovable fanaticism which inspired those who had been involved from the beginning in the English situation. And Phayre, at least, who was only twenty-nine, was an incipient administrator rather than military leader.

Also, Hercules Huncks had predominantly Royalist connections. His elder brother, Sir Fulke, had brought a regiment from Ireland to fight for the King and had been the Royalist Governor of Shrewsbury; and Hercules himself who was a born soldier had originally enlisted for the King under Lord Byron in the 'Bishop's War' against the Scots in 1640—before there was any thought of Civil War. Byron, most loyal of Cavaliers, had supported the King's cause all through the Civil War and, now in France, was tutor to the young Duke of York. Huncks, after Naseby, undertook to raise a company to fight in Ireland under Lord Lisle and had served in Munster under Lord Inchiquin. But neither Lisle (who had refused to have anything to do with the King's trial) nor Inchiquin (who had become a Parliamentarian only because that party held the command of the seas and so controlled Irish economy), was exactly dependable and Inchiquin, as soon as he had made himself master of the south of Ireland with the aid of the supplies brought by Lisle, had promptly returned to his first loyalty, declared for the King and started to fortify the Irish ports against Cromwell.

It was certainly true that Huncks, in the company of Lisle, had thereupon returned to England to assure Parliament of his loyalty to them and they on their part by their appointment of him to the Governorship of Londonderry might seem to have recognized it. But his background was obviously not altogether reassuring and Cromwell's selection of him to be responsible in a very particular manner for the King's killing might be considered as a test.

At the moment, Huncks was showing every sign of failing it.

When Daniel Axtell came back to Ireton's room to get the warrant for the executioners, who were now preparing themselves for their public appearance by donning impenetrable disguises, he found that it was still unsigned.

Cromwell held out the pen to Huncks.

Huncks refused to take it, whereupon Axtell rapped out: "Colonel Huncks, I am ashamed of you. The ship is now coming into harbour and will you strike sail before we come to anchor?"

But Huncks still pushed away the pen, saying: "Why should it be offered to me?"

"Because," said Cromwell, "you are named by virtue of the warrant, to draw up an order for the executioner."

"That is so," said Hacker, who was reading the warrant.

"The matter needs further discussion," said Huncks.

"There has been enough time wasted already," said Cromwell. "It brooks of no delay now."

Again he offered the pen to Huncks. And again Huncks refused it.

"You are a froward, peevish fellow, Colonel Huncks," said Cromwell, and without more ado went to the little table by the door, which had paper and ink on it, and scribbled the authorization. He then gave the pen to Hacker, who signed it obediently and, with Axtell, went out of the room. Cromwell, beckoning Ireton and Harrison (who was renowned for the length of his extempore prayers) to follow him, also hurried out.

It was obvious, now, that no one was interested in either Huncks or Phayre, who were left to their own devices. They chose to have nothing further to do with the day's proceedings.

The Cozening of Fairfax

Thomas Lord Fairfax (he had succeeded to the title on his father's death ten months ago) was Cromwell's last remaining problem. The relationship between the two men, never easy, was approaching a crisis. Fairfax, who was now thirty-six, was twelve years Cromwell's junior; and though he was his superior in the Army—Lord-General to Cromwell's Lieutenant-Colonel—it was becoming obvious to everyone that Cromwell was the greater soldier. But it had not always been so. Cromwell had been a quiet civilian-farmer until he was over forty; Fairfax had gone to the Continental wars with the famous volunteer regiment raised by Vere and been blooded at the siege of Bois-le-Duc when he was seventeen. He was the professional to Cromwell's amateur. When Cromwell had no thought of fighting, Fairfax held a command in the first Scottish war. As a military leader, trained in a hard school, he never lost Cromwell's respect; but it was not for that reason that young Fairfax's command of the New Model Army three years ago had been engineered. Richard Baxter, the Army chaplain, gave the reason for that when he wrote: "This man was chosen because they supposed to find him a man of no quickness of parts, of no elocution, of no suspicious plotting wit and therefore one that Cromwell could make use of at his pleasure. And he was acceptable to sober men because he was religious, faithful, valiant, and of a grave, sober, resolved disposition; very fit for execution and neither too great nor too cunning to be commanded by Parliament."

In the field, there was no doubt of 'Black Tom's' valour and ability. He never spared himself, though he suffered agonies from gout; on his face, he bore like a badge the sword-cut he received at Marston Moor; and his men loved him. It was this which distinguished him from the long line of mediocrities in history who have occupied positions of eminence merely on account of their mediocrity. Fairfax had enough real power to force his manipulators to convince him before they used him. He could neither be over-ruled nor swept aside with safety. A Yorkshireman, he arrived at his conclusions slowly and in formulating them his stammer made him appear even slower than he was. But he also had the Yorkshire stubbornness which, once he was convinced of a course of political action, made him as reluctant to abandon it as he was to abandon a position in the field.

And, at this point, there was no doubt that every day had increased and every hour was increasing his opposition to the killing of the King. Ever since his own refusal to attend the King's trial and his wife's protest at it, his energies had been directed to preventing Charles's death. Even at this last hour, with the scaffold prepared and Charles waiting to be led to it, he was insisting on discussion and delay.

It might have seemed that it was too late; practical preparations were too far advanced. Yet the idea of a mock-execution as a device to break the King's nerve was so little fantastic that many later admitted that "they could never believe his death was intended till it was too late; they thought all was a pageantry to strike terror and to force the King to such concessions as they had a mind to extort from him." And those who thought thus had a good precedent for their belief. A vivid memory to the older generation and a legend to the younger was the doing of this very thing by Charles's father, King James, forty-five years ago.

Markham, Grey, Cobham and the great Raleigh had all been condemned to death for alleged conspiracy. Markham was already kneeling at the block when a message, which King James had deliberately postponed till this last moment, arrived and he was taken back to custody, with the assurance of two hours respite. Grey, unaware of this, followed to the block, accompanied by a Puritan divine who made a long prayer, which Grey outdid with an even longer one and, according to one spectator, "held us in the rain more than half-an-hour." Then, as he laid his head on the block, he too received the news that the order of execution had been changed by royal command and that Cobham was to suffer first. But Cobham, as he knelt down, was given the same treatment. Eventually all were addressed by the Sheriff who asked: "Are not your offences heinous? Have you not been justly tried and lawfully condemned? Is not each of you subject to due execution, now to be performed?"

Not surprisingly in the circumstances, they replied in the affirmative and were all reprieved on a warrant James had signed three days before.

The elaborate farce concocted by the royal degenerate had had two effects. It justified one of the Government's more outrageous actions, since there had been only a bogus plot, fabricated by the Government itself. And it had broken Raleigh's nerve sufficiently for him to write in terms which his admirers have preferred to forget (and which, indeed, were overbalanced by his gay bravery when at last, years later, he came to the scaffold): "We have this day beheld a work of so great mercy and for so great offences, as the like hath been seldom if ever known. And although myself have not yet been brought so near the very brink of the grave, yet I trust that so great a compassion will extend itself towards me also. Only the memory of mine own unworthiness made me despair of so great a grace who otherwise beheld Pity in the face, the voice, the writing and life of my Sovereign."

Though later centuries were to forget the scaffold-trick—which, indeed, seemed to belong rather to mediaeval romance than to post-Reformation power-politics—yet its association with Raleigh had ensured that on this January day in 1649 it was still potent in men's memories. For Sir

John Eliot, who might justly be called the founder of the Parliamentary Party, had watched the execution of his hero, Raleigh, when at last he came to death and had left a description of the great man's ultimate bravery in unforgettable words. When Eliot had been done to death in the Tower, John Hampden, his disciple, had taken arms to avenge him; and when Hampden had fallen in battle, Cromwell had stepped into his place. It was a succession. And no man would have thought it very strange if Cromwell had used on James's son the mode of mental torture that James had invented.

Thus Fairfax had every reason to assume that, even at half-past one that day, Charles's fate could still be decided by argument and when Cromwell, in answer to his remonstrances, suggested that they should hold a discussion and prayer-meeting in Harrison's room he accepted with alacrity. What the Lord-General could not know was that his Lieutenant-General had given orders that, as soon as the King was dead, a servant, whom he had specially appointed for the purpose, was to come and knock on Harrison's door to inform them that the act was over.

In the opening discussions, the usual points of view were advanced. Cromwell even conceded that the death of the King would be extremely bad policy, "for he was not ignorant," he said, "what calumny that action would draw upon the Army and themselves in particular, though they did nothing therein but in obedience to Parliament." Someone proposed an immediate address to the Commons "and in the meanwhile, the King should be respited." Cromwell expressed "how glad he would be if such a thing might be effected."

"But before we proceed in so weighty a matter," he said, "let us seek God to know His mind in it."

The identification of God's will with Cromwell's policy had by this time become almost a matter of faith. In the

William Seymour, Marquis of Hertford

(By courtesy of the British Museum, London)

James Stuart, Duke of Lennox

(*By courtesy of the National Galleries of Scotland*)

mind of everyone in Harrison's room was the case of Elizabeth Poole, who for the last few weeks had been claiming their attention on this very subject. Indeed the revelations of Mrs. Poole about the 'Divine pleasure concerning the King' were a factor in the present attitude of those who thought she was in truth 'a servant of the Most High God.'

She had had a vision of 'a woman, full of imperfection, crooked, weak, sickly and imperfect' (who was obviously England) and a man 'a member of the Army, devoted to his country, its liberty and freedom which he should gladly be a sacrifice for' (which was the Army in general). The man was intended to cure the woman and would do so provided, said Mrs. Poole, "he shall, before the Lord, act diligently and faithfully to employ all means which I shall by the gift of God in me direct for her cure."

Her first revelation had been generally approved. It was that the Army leaders must "go forward and stand up for the liberty of the people as it was their liberty and God had opened the way for them." No one had been disposed to doubt that this part of the message was of Divine origin. It was when Mrs. Poole came to the second part—that they must deny themselves, because "perfectly dying in the will of the Lord, you may find your resurrection in Him" (in other words, that they must save the King's life)—that doubts had been awakened.

One of the younger Moderates, indeed, had approved the whole doctrine and pointed out that, unless their liberty was used in a way which practical men might not understand, "I believe, as she says, the conclusion of it will be but fleshly after having begun in the spirit." But the general feeling had been against her; and her answer to Harrison's question: "Is anything given you more particularly to express?"—"No, sir. It was presented to me as the Church"—was considered particularly disappointing.

When she had become even more definite and had presented a paper against the King's execution, Ireton had asked unkindly: "What would you hold forth to us as the demonstration that this that you have delivered to us is to be read as from God, from Him given to you and from you intended to be delivered to us?"

Her answer that the paper bore witness for itself had considerably weakened her case, for its arguments were hardly on the metaphysical plane and her own reply that "I do look upon the Norman Conquest, whereby kings came to reign, to be of Divine pleasure, though God is not a supporter of tyranny or injustice" differed little from the political pronunciamentos of those who laid no claim to Divine inspiration. Indeed, as another Colonel had pointed out: "God doth not send a messenger except that there may be an impression upon their hearts that are to receive it." Mrs. Poole's message "either must be from God or else there must be something of argument and reason in it. And if it be from God, we should be pleased to hear what outgoings there are in that particular." The majority, disapproving of the visionary's declaration against the King's death, had thereupon intimated their scepticism about its origin.

Yet the unanswered point remained as it had been formulated by one who had tried honestly to grapple with the difficulty: "Is not the will of God always concordant with natural reason? Is it the will of God that anything in point of government should be inconsistent with the essential being for which government was ordained? And therefore is it the will or mind of God that if a man empowered with government is tyrannous to the governed (for whose well-being he is set in the Chair), cannot this forfeiture of his trust be outwardly manifested by the forfeiture of his life?" And it was to this point that Harrison and Ireton and the rest now returned.

But Fairfax was still 'distracted in mind' as he listened to

Cromwell's harsh, untunable voice commencing 'a long-winded prayer.'

The Executioners prepare

Hacker and Axtell took the warrant to the rooms where under the supervision of Colonel Hewson the two men who had volunteered as headsman and assistant were disguising themselves for their task. The recompense of a hundred pounds and speedy promotion—William Hulet immediately afterwards jumped from sergeant to captain—had been accompanied by the promise of absolute secrecy. Without it, neither could with safety have acted for the repercussions were unpredictable; and they were unknown even to each other.

They were given close-fitting woollen frocks of a dark colour, like those worn by butchers or sailors, with frieze trunk breeches. Large black vizards impenetrably masked their faces and to complete the disguise they were provided with large wigs and false beards. The executioner's wig—a 'grey grizzled periwig'—hung very low and with the addition of a large grey beard had an effect so transforming that Hewson nicknamed him 'Father Greybeard.'

The eminent assistant to the executioner affected a black beard and wig and added to his costume a large flapped black hat, looped up in the front, which as a last insult to the King he did not intend to doff.

The executioner's chief concern, once he was satisfied with his anonymity, was with the sharpness of the axe. Whatever he might be, he had no wish to appear an amateur in public. To set his mind at rest, Captain James Berry was accordingly ordered to go to the scaffold to give his professional opinion on it. In such a matter Berry was an expert. The choice of him was, in addition, a tactful assessment of priorities. It had been quite clear to everyone since last August when Cromwell had chosen him to carry to the Speaker the news of the victory at Preston, which had ended the Second Civil War and put an end to the King's hopes, that Berry was destined for promotion, especially as on that occasion he had been given £200 by the Commons for his service.

Berry was, in fact, one of Cromwell's oldest friends. He had been an original member of the first troop of horse Oliver had raised in the Eastern Counties. In an early skirmish, he had covered himself with glory by killing the Earl of Newcastle's young brother, Charles Cavendish; and Cromwell had recounted the incident in detail in more than one letter, telling how he had forced Cavendish into a quagmire where Berry 'cut him on the head, by reason of which he fell off his horse, whereat he gave him a thrust under the short ribs whereof within two hours he died.' But Berry's knowledge of weapons was not confined to his skilful use of them. Before he had enlisted with Cromwell, he had been employed in an ironworks.

So now Hacker and Berry, taking with them Tench to have a last look at the ropes and pulleys and others to see that the little low billet of a quartering-block[1] was firm, came out on the scaffold. The party left an indelible impression on the mind of one, Benjamin Francis, who was 'coming out of Westminster into London about half-an-hour before the King came on the scaffold.' He was caught in the crowd which was so dense that he 'could not pass backward or forward but was enforced to stand there.'

[1] The block was about eighteen inches long, six inches in height, flat at the bottom and rounded at the top. It was fashioned for the decapitation of a corpse, since prisoners to be beheaded and quartered—part of the sentence for high treason—were already dead from hanging and disembowelling before this part of their punishment was carried out. Charles was thus to be beheaded not 'kneeling at the block' like Strafford and Laud, but 'lying at the block.' This explains the King's concern, when he saw it, that it was so low. It also adds point to Peters' suggestion that he should be reduced to the condition of corpse-like immobility by being bound and dragged along the scaffold.

"During that time," he said, "I saw the scaffold; and the axe and the block taken up by divers people; and principally I saw James Berry take the axe up and try it with his thumb and lay it down again."

With the verdict of Berry's connoisseurship, the executioner had to be content. Everything was now in order and Hacker went to call the King.

Hacker summons the King

In the King's apartments, Colonel Tomlinson and the guards had withdrawn to the antechamber, leaving the King alone with Juxon and Herbert. Charles was kneeling apart from the others, praying, while, as far away as possible and speaking in whispers so as not to disturb him, Herbert admitted to the Bishop that he was afraid. He could not answer for his actions any longer. On the scaffold he might disgrace himself.[1]

Fingering the white flowered night-cap which the King had chosen for the scaffold, he said: "His Majesty has ordered me to have this ready, but I am not able to endure the sight of the violence they will offer him on the scaffold."

Juxon understandingly took the cap from him and answered: "I will see to that. You can wait in the Banqueting Hall, near the scaffold-end, to take care of the King's body when it is over. That, and the burial, will be our last office."

When Hacker and his guard arrived at the outer door he was met by Tomlinson, to whom he showed the warrant.

"This means," said Tomlinson, "that my duty is at an end."

"That is so," answered Hacker. "Will you tell the King?"

"No," said Tomlinson, "neither I nor anyone here intends

[1] It is not, I think, necessary to assume—as is always done—that he was afraid of 'breaking down' merely. He was not 'an aged retainer'; he was still a comparatively young and tough man, who might have assaulted the executioner. And he was still, technically, a Cromwellian.

to tell him that orders for his safety are ended. You can do it yourself."

So Hacker went to the inner door and 'gave his last signal.'

On hearing the knock, both Juxon and Herbert "weeping fell upon their knees and the King gave them his hand to kiss; and helped the Bishop up, for he was aged." Then the door was opened.

Charles gave Hacker no chance to read the warrant. He said merely that he would be grateful if Tomlinson was allowed to come on the scaffold with him and then said composedly: "Go on. I will follow."

They went downstairs, into the cold air of the courtyard.

In the Banqueting Hall

From the courtyard an outside staircase led to the Banqueting Hall. Mounting it, Charles entered for the last time Inigo Jones's superb room, built in the proportions of a double cube, which had been the symbol of his happiness and splendour in the days of peace. No irony could have been more subtly contrived. Above him, in the glowing colours of the panelled ceiling, was himself at his accession, painted allegorically as embracing the Goddess of Wisdom and overcoming Envy and Rebellion. His last few steps to death were now to be taken under the panel showing his birth, with his father pointing at him with his sceptre to indicate that Wisdom was his nurse.

For that ceiling, which was his memorial to his father, he had paid Rubens with £3,000 and a knighthood and had so treasured it that, after the paintings had been put in position, he had prohibited any further masques in the Hall. The panels might be damaged by the elaborate cloud-machines and other apparatus. Also, the three hundred stage-hands which a Royal masque required could not be presumed to have his own careful connoisseurship; and fire was always a danger.

At the last masque which had been performed there fourteen years ago—in 1635—he and the Queen, sitting in state, had watched a great rose-tinted cloud, which was a technician's masterpiece, descend slowly and, gradually opening before it reached the ground, reveal seated in its centre a beautiful woman representing Divine Poesy. One of the scenes had satirized the Puritans in general and William Prynne, the enemy of the theatre, in particular. A 'modern devil' entered, 'a sworn enemy of poesy, music and all ingenious arts, but a great friend to murmuring, libelling and all seeds of discord, attended by his factious followers, all of which was expressed by their habits and dance.' In 1635, it had been possible to think of the faction in such simple terms and natural for young Will Davenant, whose first masque it was, to do so. Then this reputed son of William Shakespeare was little but a gay court-poet and dramatist. But, when war came, he had fought bravely enough and Charles had knighted him at the siege of Gloucester. Now Sir William Davenant, having recently risked his life to bring Charles letters from Henrietta in France, was fulfilling another errand for the Queen and preparing for a voyage to Virginia.

Yet in Davenant's last masque—the last ever to be performed at Whitehall,[1] the last in which Charles and Henrietta had danced in state—he had not hesitated to present there at Court in 1640 the worsening situation. The curtain had risen on a scene of storm and tempest. 'No glimpse of the sun was seen, as if darkness, confusion and deformity had possessed the world and driven the light from Heaven. The trees were bent as if forced by a gust of wind, their branches rent from their trunks and some torn up by the roots. Far off was a dark-wrought sea, with rolling

[1] It took place in the newly-provided Masquing Room.

billows breaking against the rocks, with rain, lightning and thunder. In the midst was a globe of the earth, which at an instant falling on fire, was turned into a Fury, her hair upright, mixed with snakes; her body lean, wrinkled and of a swarthy colour. In her hand she brandished a sable torch and looking askance with hollow, envious eyes, came down into the room.' This Fury had then invoked evil spirits to bring discord throughout England and at her summons three had entered in a wild menacing dance. Then, suddenly, the scene had changed into a landscape, showing a country at peace, rich and fruitful. Out of the heavens had come in a silver chariot Concord, a woman, accompanied by the Good Genius of Great Britain, a young man in a vivid red silk costume—the very colour of the striped waistcoat that the King was wearing now. Together they had recited for Charles:

> O, who but he could thus endure
> To live and govern in a sullen age,
> When it is harder far to cure
> The people's folly than resist their rage?

After a series of dances in which the forces of discord were variously represented, the scene had changed once more into 'craggy rocks and inaccessible mountains. In the upper parts where any earth could fasten were some trees, but of strange forms such as only grow in remote parts of the Alps and in desolate places. The farthest of these was hollow in the midst and so high that the top pierced the clouds. All this represented the difficult way which heroes must pass before they come to the Throne of Honour.'

That throne was for Charles. Suddenly the central rock had opened and revealed him seated upon it. Then a great cloud of various colours had come down from the sky, obliterating in its descent the Throne of Honour, and bearing in it Henrietta dressed as an Amazon, in the same vivid red embroidered with silver, with a plumed helmet and an antique sword. Charles had then gone to his wife's side and together the tiny couple had danced gravely down the room.

The Banqueting Hall was still crowded, though soldiers now lined the spaces between the pillars where once courtiers and ambassadors had taken their places in correct precedence. Behind the picked Ironsides, on guard against a last-minute attempt at rescue, 'abundance of men and women crowded in, though with some peril to their persons, to behold the saddest sight England ever saw'—the words are Herbert's—'and as His Majesty passed by, with a cheerful look, he heard them pray for him, the soldiers not rebuking any of them; by their silence and dejected faces seeming afflicted rather than insulting."

Those who watched now were, most of them, the servants and staff of Whitehall Palace, sharing the King's memories of the gaiety of but a few years ago. The eighteen-year-old Philip Henry, who, in childhood, had played with the young Princes, was in the crowded street, but his father, John, who had been one of Charles's own pages and still had apartments in the Palace, was there. The King, who had supposed he was dead, had spoken delightedly to him a few days earlier at the time of the trial.

In silence now, he watched his master walk the length of the hall with as firm a step and as light a countenance as if he were still at a masque, though the cloud-capp'd towers and gorgeous palaces of the insubstantial pageant had long faded, leaving behind only a hole made in the wall to give access to the room beyond where a window led to a scaffold.

The Scaffold

On the north—the Charing Cross—side of the Banqueting House was a small building with a sloping roof, two storeys high and the width of a single room. With its low-walled yard, where in the corner a tree grew, it occupied the space between the Hall and the square-turreted Gatehouse over the arch of the public gate of Whitehall Palace. Its lower window was on a level with those of the Banqueting Hall and, though smaller, was large enough, when the frame was removed, to allow an easy passage to the scaffold which had been erected outside it.

This building which was in the nature of an annexe had survived the fire of 1619, which had burnt down the old Banqueting House and made way for Inigo Jones's new architectural masterpiece and the window that now led to the scaffold was the same which, in 1614, when Charles was a boy of fourteen, had led to an earlier scaffold erected for a great display of fencing. Charles's maternal uncle, King Christian of Denmark, had been on a visit to England and for his amusement all the fencers of London 'had encountered each other in their school way.' That scaffold served as a model for this, except that this was slightly larger—a projecting oblong which in width extended as far as the second window of the Banqueting Hall and in length reached even further out into the road.

From the road it was impossible to see on to the scaffold itself now that the railings round it had been hung with black cloth. Only the spectators at the upper windows and on the roofs of the surrounding buildings could see the block and the ropes and pulleys and the cheap little deal coffin.

The King, with Juxon by his side, preceded by Hacker, and the guard of soldiers, and followed by some shorthand reporters, came through the window and 'strode the floor of death with a cheerful countenance.' But he was momentarily dismayed at seeing how low the block was and asked Hacker if there was no higher one. Hacker said there was not. Charles then looked at the dense throngs of spectators and realized they were too far away to hear his dying speech. That was intended. But he would address the fifteen people round him on the scaffold. Taking from his pocket the 'small piece of paper some four inches square' on which he had written some notes, he started his last speech to the nation and posterity. It was nearly two o'clock. For the first time that day, the sun broke through the clouds and shone brilliantly. Interpret it as they might, none of the thousands who saw it could escape the significance of the phenomenon and an unknown poet in the crowd interpreted it as a symbol of the King himself:

> Nor mask, nor veil, nor sables would it wear,
> Nor red with anger, nor yet pale with fear.

The King's Speech

"I shall be very little heard of anybody here. I shall therefore speak a word unto you here," said the King, turning to speak directly to Colonel Tomlinson, who was standing close to the window and could hardly be said to be on the scaffold at all.

"Indeed I could hold my peace very well, if I did not think that holding my peace would make some men think I did submit to the guilt as well as the punishment. But I think it is my duty to God first and to my country for to clear myself both as an honest man and a good King and a good Christian.

"I shall begin first with my innocency. In troth I think it is not very needful for me to insist long upon this, for all the world knows that I never did begin a war with the two Houses of Parliament. And I call God to witness, to whom I must shortly make an account, that I never did intend for to encroach upon their privileges. They began upon me. It is the Militia they began upon. They confessed that the Militia was mine, but they thought it fit to have it from me.

"And, to be short, if anybody will look to the dates of the Commissions—of their commissions and mine—and likewise to the Declarations, he will see clearly that they began these unhappy troubles, not I. So that as the guilt of these enormous crimes that are laid against me I hope in God that God will clear me of it. I will not. (I am in charity.) God forbid that I should lay it upon the two Houses of Parliament; there is no necessity of either. I hope that they are free of this guilt. For I do believe that ill instruments between them and me have been the chief cause of all this bloodshed. So that, by way of speaking, as I find myself clear of this, I hope (and pray God) that they may too. Yet, for all this, God forbid that I should be so ill a Christian as not to say God's judgments are just upon me. Many times He does pay justice by an unjust sentence. That is ordinary. I will only say that an unjust sentence that I suffered for to take effect is punished now by an unjust sentence upon me."

The death of Strafford had long been on Charles's conscience. He had given Strafford his word that he would not give assent to the Bill of Attainder by which the Commons, in 1641, had determined to bring the great Royalist statesman to death. Against riots and rumours inflaming public opinion, he had held out. Even when Strafford himself gave the King quittance and wrote from the Tower releasing him from his promise, Charles had still held on. But, after the Third Reading of the Bill, the Constable of the Tower declared that if the King still refused to sign he would kill the prisoner on his own authority; John Pym, the architect of Strafford's death, let it be known that, were he baulked of it, he would impeach the Queen, and the London mob, inflamed by Pym's agents, gathered round Whitehall, where the Queen and her attendants, having made their confessions, waited with what courage they could muster for the violation and murder they thought inevitable.

Charles had sent for five bishops to counsel him. The majority were of the opinion that he might break his word on the principle that, as the future Archbishop of York put it, "the King has two consciences, a public one and a private one." But grim old James Ussher, Primate of Ireland, relentlessly opposed such a quibble and William Juxon was equally uncompromising: "Sir, if your conscience is against it, do not consent."

Throughout that terrible Sunday, with the mob's cries for the Queen monotonously rising outside and the guard, hastily summoned from St. James's, preparing to defend her in case of attack, Charles had still hesitated between the two opinions. At last he had signed, explaining to the Privy Council: "If my own person only were in danger, I would gladly venture it to save Lord Strafford's life but, seeing my wife, children and all my kingdom are concerned in it, I am forced to give way," and adding: "Lord Strafford's condition is happier than mine."

Now that he was about to share Strafford's fate and everything was lost more irrevocably than it would have been had Strafford lived, Charles made this public acknowledgment of his fault. It was to Juxon that he spoke. But Ussher, too, was watching the scene from the roof of Wallingford House just across the road. Already he was feeling faint and, in a few moments, had to be taken below.

"What I have said so far," the King continued, "is to show you I am an innocent man. Now for to show you that I am a good Christian. I hope that this good man here"—he pointed to Juxon—"will bear witness that I have forgiven all the world and even those in particular that have been the chief causes of my death. Who they are God knows. I do not desire to know. God forgive them. But this is not all. My charity must go further. I wish that they may repent, for indeed they have committed a great sin in that particular. I pray God with St. Stephen that this be not laid to their charge. Nay, not only so, but that they may take the right way to the peace of the kingdom, for my charity commands me not only to forgive particular men, but my charity commands me to endeavour to the last gasp the peace of the kingdom. So, Sirs, I do wish with all my soul and I do hope that there are some here"—Charles turned towards the shorthand-writers—"who will carry it further that they may endeavour the peace of the kingdom.

"Now, Sirs, I must show you both how you are out of the way and will put you in a way.

"First, you are out of the way, for certainly all the way you have ever had yet, as I could find by anything, is by way of conquest. Certainly this is an ill way, for conquest, Sir, in my opinion is never just, except there be a good, just cause, either for matter of wrong or just title. And then, if you go beyond it, the first quarrel that you have to it makes unjust at the end what was just at the beginning. But if it be only a matter of conquest, there is a great robbery. As a pirate said to Alexander, he was a great robber whereas himself was but a petty robber. And so, Sir, I do think the way you are in is much out of the way.

"Now, Sir, for to put you in the way. Believe it, you will never do right, nor God will never prosper you, until you give God His due, the King his due (that is, my successors) and the people their due. I am as much for them as any of you. You must give God His due by regulating rightly His Church (according to the Scripture) which is now out of order. For to set you in a way particularly now I cannot, but only this. A national synod freely called, freely debating among themselves, must settle this, when every opinion is freely and clearly heard.

"For the King, indeed, I will not——"

He broke off suddenly. One of the bystanders had touched the axe. Charles was afraid that the edge would be blunted and so give him needless pain. He could not forget how his grandmother, Mary, Queen of Scots, had been hacked to death by blow after blow on the scaffold at Fotheringhay. "Hurt not the axe," he said, "that it may not hurt me."

Resuming his speech, he said: "For the King, the laws of the land will clearly instruct you for that. Therefore, because it concerns my own particular, I only touch on it.

"For the people, truly I desire their liberty and freedom as much as anybody whomsoever. But I must tell you their liberty and freedom consists in having government—those laws by which their life and their goods may be most their own. It is not having a share in government. That is nothing pertaining to them. A subject and a sovereign are clean different things and therefore, until they do that—I mean that you do put the people in that liberty as I say—certainly they will never enjoy themselves.

"Sirs, it is for this that I am now come here. If I would have given way to an arbitrary power, for to have all laws changed according to the power of the sword, I need not have come here. And therefore I tell you—and I pray God it be not laid to your charge—that I am the martyr of the people.

"In troth, sirs, I shall not hold you much longer. I will only say this to you—that in truth I could have desired some little time longer, because I could then have put what I have said in a little more order and a little better digested than I have done. And therefore I hope you will excuse me.

"I have delivered my conscience. I pray God that you do take those courses that are best for the good of the kingdom and for your own salvations."

When he had ended, Juxon reminded him that there was one thing which he had not explicitly stated. "Will your Majesty," said the Bishop, "though it may be very well known—Your Majesty's affections towards religion—yet it may be expected that you should say somewhat for the world's satisfaction?"

"I thank you very heartily, my Lord," said Charles, "for that I had almost forgotten it." Addressing himself once more to those on the scaffold, he added: "In troth, sirs, my conscience in religion is, I think, very well known to all the world, and therefore I declare before you all that I die a Christian according to the profession of the Church of England as I found it left me by my father. And this honest man"—he indicated Juxon—"I think will witness it."

Then, turning to the Puritan officers, he added: "Sirs, excuse me for this same. I have a good cause and I have a gracious God. I will say no more."

The Execution

There was no more to say. All that remained were the final preparations for death. Charles looked again, steadily and carefully, at the instruments of the ritual. Once more, disconcerted by the lowness of the block, he asked if it were not possible to have one at which he might kneel in the usual fashion. Hacker repeated that it was impossible. Search had been made when the axe was brought from the Tower, but no such block could be found.

"Then see it is set fast," said the King.

They demonstrated to him that it was set fast enough; but, in the process the axe was in danger of being knocked over and blunted, and the King's old fear momentarily returned. "Have a care of the axe," he said again.

But when he looked at the ropes and pulleys, his composure had returned. 'He took no notice of some engines his murderers had made that in case he would not willingly submit they might by violence have pulled him down; at which he smiled, as if he had been contented that they showed the barbarity of their natures and he the equanimity of his own.'

He took off his cloak and his George, which he gave to Juxon, with the one word, pronounced loudly and clearly so that everyone on the scaffold heard it: "Remember." To the Bishop too he gave his gold ring, and the small prayer-book he had used for the last ten years at his bedside, which he had brought with him to the scaffold.[1]

Juxon, doing Herbert's duty, handed him the white cap. Charles, having put up his long curls under it so that his neck might be left bare, asked the executioner: "Is any of my hair in the way now?"

"I beg you to push it more under your cap," said the man.

As Juxon's old fingers helped to make the adjustment, the Bishop said in a low voice: "You have but one stage more. It is turbulent and troublesome, but it is a short one, though it will carry you a very great way. It will carry you from earth to heaven."

Charles caught the echo of his Coronation sermon. "I am going," he answered, "from a corruptible to an incorruptible crown, where no disturbance can be." The intolerably troubled interim of living was over. "No disturbance in the world."

The King then took off his doublet, but, still afraid of appearing afraid in the cold, he took his cloak again and wrapped it round him.

As the executioner fell on his knees and asked for pardon, Sergeant Gittens, who was on guard by the scaffold and had noticed Hulet's absence, suddenly recognized Hulet's voice. But Charles could not give the pardon. As man to man, indeed, he had forgiven all his enemies; but in this particular action the whole principle for which he was dying was involved. To have pronounced pardon would have nullified his stubborn death. He, the source of law, could not authorize the ultimate lawlessness of high treason. The simple, conventional request of the headsman, made at a moment of such high emotion, was the last and most deadly trap.

"The King cannot pardon a subject who wilfully sheds his

[1] This prayer book eventually came into the possession of John Evelyn and on the fly-leaf in Evelyn's handwriting: "This is the Booke which Charles the First M.B." (Martyr Beatus) "did use upon the Scaffold xxx Jan. 1648, being the day of his glorious martyrdom."

blood," Charles answered; then added quickly, implicitly restoring the humanity of the situation: "I pray you, do not put me to pain."

The King moved to the edge of the scaffold and for a moment it seemed that he was about, after all, to make an attempt to speak to the tight-wedged, silent crowd. But he only looked—as those in the street noticed—toward St. James's and smiled.

Then he spoke again to the executioner: "I shall say but a short prayer and, when I hold out my hands thus, strike."

For a minute or two he stood in profound meditation. Then he murmured to himself a few inaudible words before he lay down with his head over the block and could no longer be seen by the spectators in the street. They saw nothing but the flash of the upraised axe before it crashed down and killed the King at its first falling.

Young Philip Henry in the crowd left it on record: "At the instant when the blow was given there was such a dismal universal groan amongst the thousands of people who were in sight of it as it were with one consent, as I never heard before and desire I may never hear again."

The assistant to the executioner picked up the head and held it high for all to see. There was a sudden silence. But the man did not cry out as he had been instructed and as the crowd anticipated: "Behold the head of a traitor." Men thought it very strange that he said nothing at all.

But the one thing that Hugh Peters dared not do was to let anyone hear his voice. That was the penalty of his notoriety, for no one, either on the scaffold or round it, could have mistaken his well-known, sonorous tones. To have spoken would have been tantamount to stripping himself publicly of his disguise. Peters vented his feelings by throwing Charles's head down on the scaffold with such violence that the still-warm cheek was badly bruised.

Afterwards

The scaffold, once death was accomplished, became a booth. Those who from piety or hatred or curiosity wished to dip their handkerchiefs in the King's blood were admitted for money. Pieces of the boards which the blood had soaked and handfuls of sand which had been scattered on it to dry it were sold at prices adjusted to the computed means of their buyers. "The soldiers took of some a shilling, of others half a crown, more or less according to the persons that sought it," one journalist reported, "but none without ready money." The soldiers on duty dipped their swords in the blood and, seeing a market, stained sticks and hands with it. Charles's hair was cut off, until at the back it was only an inch long. As another spectator recorded: "They were inhumanly barbarous to his dead corpse. His hair and his blood were sold by parcels. Their hands and sticks were tinged by his blood and the block, now cut into chips, as also the sand sprinkled with his sacred gore, were exposed for sale. Which were greedily bought, but for different ends; by some as trophies of their slain enemy and by others as precious relics of their beloved prince." One soldier was overheard saying to another: "I would we had two or three more Majestys to behead, if we could but make such use of them."

But at last the knot round the scaffold dwindled, for the main body of spectators who had been jammed so tightly that it was impossible to move were scattered by the two troops of horse—the one on guard at the Holbein Gate moving north and passing that stationed at Charing Cross moving south. The street was thus expeditiously cleared, except for the souvenir-hunters fringing the scaffold. But within the grounds of the palace, there was still a curious, aimless crowd, wandering and wondering what the next move would be.

In this crowd was Abraham Smith, a waterman, who suddenly found himself confronted by a file of musketeers accompanying Brandon, the public hangman. Immediately the execution was over, Brandon had been released from his captivity, given forty half-crowns as compensation for his detention and told he would be taken home in safety by one of the official barges.

"Where are the bargemen?" the sergeant in charge of the musketeers asked Smith, seeing by his badge that he was a waterman.

"There are none about," said Smith.

"Then we shall use your boat," said the sergeant. "Take us to it."

Smith dared not refuse, though he had recognized—or thought he had recognized—the identity of his enforced passenger. When they got to the waterside, Brandon gave the sergeant half a crown for his pains and the sergeant ordered Smith: "Waterman, get him away as quickly as you can."

Abraham Smith was panic-stricken. "I, fearing this was the hangman that had cut off the King's head," he reported later, "I trembled that he should come into my boat, but dared not to examine him on shore for fear of the soldiers. So out I launched and having got a little way in the water, said I: 'Who the devil have I got in my boat?' "

"Why do you want to know?" said Brandon.

Smith shot at him: "Aren't you the hangman that has just cut off the King's head?"

"No," said Brandon, "as I am a sinner before God, I did not do it."

By now it was the hangman who was trembling though in face of his denial, Abraham Smith was at a loss what to do next.

He decided to row out into mid-stream, saying nothing more but looking at Brandon quizzically. At last, when they were isolated on the river with no one in hailing distance, he spoke again.

"Can you swim?"

Brandon shook his head.

"Then," said Smith, "I am going to sink this boat here unless you tell me the truth, for I refuse to carry you if you are the hangman who cut off the King's head."

Brandon, realizing that Smith was in earnest, decided that only the truth could save him.

"Yes," he said, still trembling a little, "I am Brandon, the hangman; but I did not do the deed." He then explained how he had been fetched from his home early in the morning and taken to Whitehall and how, on his refusal, he had been kept under guard until a moment or two before Smith met him. "But they had my instruments," he admitted.

The waterman continued with his questions interspersed by renewed threats to sink the boat until, convinced by Brandon's honesty, he undertook to row him safely to the steps by the Tower, in return for adequate payment, which Brandon made in half-crowns.

Meanwhile, on the scaffold, the body of the King had at last been laid in the cheap deal coffin standing there to receive it and, attended by Herbert and Juxon, it was taken to the back-stairs to await the arrival of Dr. Thomas Trappam, Surgeon-General to the Senior Parliamentary officers, who had been entrusted with the embalming of it. Then, since there was nothing they could do until Trappam had finished his work, they returned slowly to the room in the Long Gallery.

As they entered the Gallery, they were surprised to meet Fairfax and still more surprised to hear him ask them how the King was. They thought they had not heard aright, but, as he repeated the question, they assumed that for some reason he was unaware of the execution and informed him that the King was dead.

Fairfax, realizing that the Prayer Meeting which he had just left had been a trap to immobilize him, stammered his consternation and hurried away, determining from that moment to break with his associates.

He was hardly out of sight before Cromwell came into the Gallery from another room at the further end, and, as he passed Herbert and Juxon, he told them that orders for the King's burial would be given them as soon as possible. Then, with Bowtell, an acquaintance from East Anglia, who had called on him on this auspicious day, Oliver went quickly to satisfy himself that Charles was dead before he attended the afternoon session of the House of Commons, for which Members were already assembling.

The coffin was still waiting at the top of the back-stairs. Cromwell tried to open the side with his staff, but it had been well closed and he found that he could not move it. He thereupon took Bowtell's sword from him and knocked the lid up with the pummell. For a moment Cromwell looked at the dead King, who was smiling serenely as if he were giving audience; then, with a gesture which was a manifestation partly of his detached curiosity and partly of his physical cruelty, he "did with his fingers search the wound as if he had still doubted of the effecting" of the execution.

Bowtell, watching Oliver, asked him what Government England would now have.

"The same that is now," said Cromwell curtly; and set out for the House of Commons to ensure it.

The Commons meet again

Even while the streets were being cleared of spectators, the House of Commons met and resumed its session. There was one matter of outstanding urgency—The Third Reading of the Bill to prevent the proclamation as King of Charles II, which had been introduced and given its Second Reading the previous day. It was now finally and unanimously passed and the Commons additionally ordered that it be 'forthwith printed and published' and that 'the Act, intituled *An Act prohibiting the proclaiming any Person to be King of England or Ireland or the Dominions thereof* be forthwith proclaimed by Sergeant Dendy, Serjeant-at-Arms, with sound of trumpet in Cheapside, the Old Exchange and Westminster.'

London was unlikely to give any trouble but there was the danger that, in parts of the country accounts of the execution might arouse sufficient sympathy to be the harbinger of trouble, so the House prudently enacted that no outgoing posts were to be allowed to leave the capital till ten o'clock next day. As, by this simple expedient, no one outside London would be in a position to know that the King was dead, the danger of any regional proclamation of his successor was thus economically averted. In the meantime, letters would be sent by the fastest Government posts to all the Sheriffs of England and Wales ordering them to proclaim the new Act "in all market towns and other public places within their several Counties and to give to this House a speedy account thereof."

The composition of this covering letter was entrusted to a Committee of two, the lawyers, John Lisle and Nicholas Love. Both had been concerned in the trial of the King, though Love had not signed the death-warrant. They were fellow M.Ps. for Winchester, both in their early forties. Both had grown rich on Hampshire Church property. Lisle, a close friend of Cromwell, had also appropriated for himself the revenues of the great charitable foundation, St. Cross, the oldest almshouse in England. Love, whose father had been one of James I's chaplains, was Recorder of Basingstoke, and had also been given the highly lucrative post of a Clerk in Chancery.[1] Together the two represented the younger generation of unscrupulous Puritan lawyers who, bent on making their fortunes, could be trusted to give the illegal an appearance of legality. And while they withdrew to frame the letter as quickly as possible—for it must obviously be dispatched to all parts of England before night—the Commons turned to discuss the topic of legality in its wider aspect.

By what right had they tried and executed the King? This simple question was now likely to be asked at every level throughout Europe. The Commons had, of course, had to answer it to their own satisfaction as a preliminary to setting up the High Court for Charles's trial and for the last three weeks they had been familiar enough with their own solution. But it was doubtful whether the generality of people even in England were aware of their theory and foreign critics would quite certainly be in complete ignorance of it.

The House therefore decided to order the printing and circulation of the three resolutions which had been drawn up by the special Committee of which Cromwell was a member on January 4 and which had since been given the force of an act.

These resolutions which, virtually conceding the principles for which the Levellers stood, were to provide posterity with a pattern for democratic republicanism, were: That the People are, under God, the origin of all just power; That the Commons of England in Parliament assembled, being chosen by and representing the People, have the supreme power in this nation: and, That whatsoever is enacted or declared for Law by the Commons in Parliament assembled, hath the force of a Law, though the concurrence of the King or the House of Peers, be not had thereto.

Given these premisses, the absurdity of arraigning a King

[1] He had made £20,000 (in the currency of the time) out of it before he fled abroad at the Restoration.

for 'High Treason' had vanished and it became logical enough to cite as an example of treason 'that Charles Stuart, not content with the many encroachments which his predecessors had made upon the people in their rights and freedoms, had a wicked design totally to subvert the ancient and fundamental laws and liberties of this nation and, in their place, to introduce an arbitrary and tyrannical government.'

In the publication and wide distribution of the Three Resolutions, the House was doing more than merely justifying its action in killing the King. It was by implication answering the King's speech on the scaffold. To Charles's: "A subject and a sovereign are clean different things," it was retorting: "Of course they are. A sovereign is merely the servant of his subjects."

Revolutions, however, do not depend for their success on Resolutions, however logical, and the Commons had no illusions about 'the people' they had elevated to sovereignty. Comfort took precedence of constitutional status. The House turned immediately to practical measures. In the morning, Members had realized for themselves how cold it was and now in the afternoon, they ordered "that the Lord Mayor and Common Council of the City of London be required to take special care that the poor of the City of London be provided for with coals at reasonable rates; and that the Justices of the Peace within the City of Westminster the Liberties thereof do take the like care for the poor within the said City of Westminster."

This, however, was a mere bagatelle. What was of overwhelming seriousness was the general financial situation, now that there was no Court to indict for extravagance and the Army's pay was hopelessly in arrears. The 'Committee who are to consider of the state of the public Monies and Treasure, or any three of them' were consequently ordered to meet and make a report within thirty-six hours and were allowed "to call in such persons as they think fit to advise them to assist them in their work."

By the time these matters were settled John Lisle and Nicholas Love had returned with the letter they had drawn up. The scriveners, inspired by the sense of urgency, had provided the requisite number of copies, which were now signed by the Speaker and given to the Solicitor-General 'to be sent to the several Sheriffs by the post.'

There remained one more thing to do. Now that there was no King and the basis of the Constitution had been altered, it was necessary to bring old legislation into line with the new theories. An Act for repealing former Acts which throughout the prolonged negotiations of the last years had assumed and admitted the Kingship had been given its First Reading the day before. This was now given its Second and referred to a Committee, which though Cromwell himself was the leading member, was composed mainly of lawyers—Lisle and Love were naturally called on again to serve with the more important luminaries—Sir Edmond Prideaux, the Solicitor-General, and Francis Thorpe, Judge of the Northern Circuit, and Sir Thomas Widdrington who was to be appointed Serjeant for the Commonwealth and Cornelius Holland, who had drawn up the charges against the King, and Bulstrode Whitelock who, though he had refused to have anything to do with the King's trial, had managed the prosecution of Strafford and was to be Cromwell's Keeper of the Great Seal. There were twenty-seven of them in all, of whom eight could form a quorum. They were to meet in the Queen's Court on Thursday, until which day the House itself now adjourned.

The Commissioners' Business

In the Painted Chamber, the attendance, which had usually been between sixty and seventy, fell that afternoon to thirteen. Those present were the little knot of men, mostly soldiers, who had tended to form a group sitting together—Thomas Scott and Simon Meyne, the two M.Ps. for Aylesbury; John Okey and John Hewson and Richard Deane and Valentine Wauton, Cromwell's brother-in-law, and Edmund Ludlow, all seasoned Colonels, with two others, Owen Rowe, the haberdasher, and Robert Tichborne, the linen-draper, who had discovered an aptitude for war which had given them social advancement. With them were John Carew, the republican with great estates in Cornwall; James Temple, the Governor of Tilbury Fort; Francis Allen, a Captain whose contribution to Army debates had showed him also an orator;[1] and Cornelius Holland, who was the only one who had not signed the King's death-warrant but whose loyalty was unquestioned.

None of the thirteen, with the exception of Wauton—and he only by reason of his relationship with Cromwell—could be considered of the first importance; but they were adequate for the straightforward and simple piece of business to be done. That business, indeed, was of such a nature that the absence of the great majority might even be regarded as evidence of tact. For all that was required was to set in motion the necessary machinery for reimbursing the whole body of regicides for their time and trouble. The thirteen appointed themselves as a Committee for this purpose. With Tichborne as chairman and a quorum of four they empowered themselves "to issue forth warrants under five of their hands to Captain John Blackwell for disbursing and payment of such sums of money as they shall think fit for the

[1] Abbot identifies him with the Francis Allen who was an Alderman of London; but the lists of Commissioners in Bradshawe's 'Journal' make no mention of this. Such an omission is not, of course, conclusive evidence, but since they are careful to specify that Andrewes and Pennington, for example, were Aldermen, the presumption, I think, must be that the regicide was the Captain Francis Allen of Ingoldsby's regiment who spoke at the Army Council of November 1, 1647, proposing that the King and the Lords should be deprived of the right of veto.

service of this Court." That done, they adjourned 'till the morrow.'

A Visitor

Major Purbeck Temple had been, four years earlier, under an obligation to Cromwell. In the preliminary manœuvres of the campaign which had culminated in Naseby, an important northern outpost of Oxford was Bletchington House, the property of Sir Thomas Coggin. It was strongly fortified and held for Charles by young Colonel Windebank in command of a garrison of two hundred men. But when Cromwell marched against it, as part of his strategy to confine the King to Oxford, Windebank, influenced, so it was reported, by his frightened wife, surrendered immediately (and, on his return to Oxford, was hanged for his cowardice).

The loss of Bletchington House, quite apart from the three hundred muskets and eighty horses which were left there as spoil for the Parliamentarians, was a severe blow to the King, since it upset his plans for leaving Oxford for the west—a move on which his grand strategy depended. Nor had Cromwell underrated the importance of the place he had won without a struggle and secured as the new Governor of it Major Purbeck Temple, whom he considered 'very right, forward and noble.'

But the changes that had taken place in the years between Naseby and now, had sent Purbeck Temple over to the King's side and this afternoon he "received an importunate command from a lady of great honour (a servant of His Majesty's)," whose name he was discreet enough never to divulge,[1] to find out where the King's body was and to bring her a description of it.

[1] It seems probable that it was the lady to whom he had sent Herbert with his ring to get the jewels just before his death—that is to say, either Lady Wheeler, the King's Laundress or Jane Whorwood who had been, if not actually Charles's mistress at Carisbrooke, a most intimate friend. In a marginal note in Herbert's own handwriting in the MSS. of his *Memoirs* he identifies the

Temple went off to Whitehall but, he admitted ruefully "after two or three score entreaties, I was denied." In his innocence, he had not realized the necessity of bribing the soldiers on guard. At last, however, the true state of affairs dawned on him and "understanding that money would do it, I gave the person then under the command of Colonel Axtell, half a piece to show it to me."

The soldiers then took Purbeck Temple to where the King's body still lay awaiting embalming. "If you think there is any sanctity or holiness in it," he said rudely, "look at it."

Temple looked, but with different eyes from Axtell's subordinate: "I saw," he said later, "the head of that blessed, martyred King lie in a coffin with his body which smiled as perfectly as if it had been alive."

The Embalming

Dr. Trappam, on the other hand, when he started embalming the body was free from any emotion except scientific curiosity. It was not the kind of work that a Maidstone practitioner, even though he had risen to be Surgeon-General to Fairfax, was often called upon to perform and it gave him a rare opportunity of practical experiment. As speed was required, there was only one method open to him. The more elaborate—and the more usual—

lady from whom he fetched the jewels as Jane Whorwood. But in a note to Sir William Dugdale written in 1681, Herbert wrote: "It was not Jane Whorwood to whom I gave the ring His Majesty sent to me" and identified her as "wife to Sir William Wheeler, the King's Laundress." Captain C. W. Firebrace's theory about this change is that possibly for some reason Jane Whorwood had asked Lady Wheeler to deputize for her. It is also, of course, possible that Jane Whorwood's name was omitted from the printed version of the *Memoirs* (where she is identified as Lady Wheeler) lest any breath of scandal should cloud Charles's name. But the Firebrace Letters and the Hopkins Letters make quite clear the intense affection between the King and Mrs. Whorwood and Captain Firebrace (*Honest Harry*, p. 192) is undoubtedly right when he says that she "was his most intimate friend and it is to her that he would have wished to send the ring as a last remembrance of him." It seems to me, therefore, that it was probably Jane Whorwood who asked Temple to bring her a description of the King's body.

operation required days to finish; but, because of the circumstances of the case, his work had to be completed by nightfall.[1]

First he removed from the body all those parts 'disposed to corruption,' and in doing so he discovered "that no man ever had all his vital parts so perfect and unhurt: and that he seemed to be of so admirable a composition and constitution that he would probably have lived as long as nature could subsist."

Dr. Trappam then applied his skill to the severed head, following the instruction that 'after emptying the cavities, surgeons ought to work at the head.' The fact that the head was already separated from the trunk made his work here the easier. He drained off the blood, sawed the cranium to take out the brain, washed the cavity with aromatic wine and filled it with the powder he had prepared and with cotton and tow soaked in liquid balsam. He then sewed up with needle and thread the skin he had incised and left the head aside until he had given the body a similar treatment. He cut the veins and arteries to rid the corpse of all blood and humidity, filling all the spaces with the powders of aloe and myrrh, and taking every care to absorb all possible moisture by drying it with a sponge before rubbing it with the liquid balsam and bandaging it with tight linen bandages which too had been soaked in the preserving liniment. Only when the work was finished and the little body clothed in its last vestment did Dr. Trappam sew the head on.

"I have," he said, "sewn on the head of a goose."

Speech after silence

Dr. Juxon, while the embalming was in process, was taken for questioning before the Council of Officers. They were

[1] No real scientific advance in methods of embalming had been made since the earliest times. Ruysch of Amsterdam, whose experiments marked a radical change in process, was not born till 1665.

anxious to know what the King had meant by his last word to the Bishop: 'Remember!' They also wanted the notes of Charles's speech which they had seen him hand to Juxon when it was over.

The Bishop fumbled in his pocket for the little four-inch square of paper, but "because of the depth of his pocket, smallness of that paper and the mixture of others therewith, could not so soon produce it as required." The officers grew impatient, suspecting a trick on the part of the old man and when at last he found it told him brutally that it was not the same one that the King had given him. Juxon protested that it was, but found himself disbelieved. Just as they were about to search him, one of the soldiers who had been on guard on the scaffold intervened. This man, when the King had started his speech, had looked carefully at the notes and now, to Juxon's relief, the "soldier whose rudeness (the bad cause of a good effect) had formerly over-inspected it in the King's hand, attested this the very same paper and prevented further suspicions which might have terminated to the Bishop's trouble." The last thing Juxon wanted was to have the other papers in his pocket inspected.

Next Ireton asked for the George, as well as the Garter which the King had forgotten to remove and was still wearing when he was beheaded. Juxon, as he handed them over, explained that the King had wished them to be sent to the Prince of Wales. Ireton, examining the medallion of St. George but not finding the secret spring which removed a plate ornamented with lilies to reveal a miniature of Henrietta Maria, merely answered that it was for Parliament to say what would be done with them. Until the will of the Commons was known, he would keep them. He would also take charge of the seals which the King had bequeathed to Princess Elizabeth. . . . And when Charles Stuart gave his George to Juxon, so Ireton understood and those who had been on the scaffold confirmed, he had said loudly the single word: 'Remember.' . . . Would the Bishop kindly inform them as to its significance? . . . Remember what?

"Just before His Majesty stepped on the scaffold," answered the Bishop, "he charged me to carry his George to Prince Charles and to command him that he should forgive his father's murderers and to charge him, if ever he came to the crown, that he should so govern his subjects as not to force them to extremities."

"And this is what he wished you to remember?"

"So I take it."

The officers were not satisfied that it was so simple. There must, they thought, be some other and hidden meaning. But Juxon could not be shaken and at last they let him go, warning him, however, that he was still to consider himself under arrest.

But there was another and far more important paper in Juxon's pocket to which the King's injunction was much more likely to refer and which must somehow be published.[1] Ever since the day when the King had not been allowed to speak after sentence at his trial, his over-riding anxiety had been that his case should somehow be presented to his people. The care that he had taken over his scaffold-speech; his discussions of it beforehand with Herbert and Tomlinson; the emphasis of his delivery of it so that the shorthand-reporters could get it down were other reflections of his preoccupation. And, to-day, only when he had actually come on to the scaffold had he realized that no one but those immediately about him would be able to hear a word he

[1] It was published on the following Monday (Thomason Tract 669, f. 13 (81)). That this was the subject of the 'Remember' and that it was in Juxon's possession is only my conjecture; but, as I trust the reader will agree, this fits the facts better than other explanations hitherto advanced. There was no one but Juxon to whom it could have been safely entrusted (since both Herbert and Tomlinson were technically Cromwellians), and it could hardly have been left at St. James's which was now open for anyone to search. The only safe place would be in Juxon's pocket—where we know there were papers which, if discovered, would have led to 'trouble.'

Thomas Wriothesley, Earl of Southampton

(By courtesy of the National Portrait Gallery, London)

Montague Bertie, Earl of Lindsey

said. His enemies who had stifled his defence in Westminster Hall had thwarted him here too. But, after the first day of his trial, he had written out the speech he intended to make on the second and it was this speech, containing the essence of all, that Juxon now had in some way to deliver to the nation.

When the Bishop explained to Ireton the meaning of 'Remember,' he was telling the truth. What he had reported, Charles had said. But he was not telling the whole truth—as, by every law of moral theology he had no need to (was, indeed, it might be argued, forbidden to) in the circumstances. For there was no particular urgency in the messages to the Prince which had been given at much greater length in the letter that Seymour would take to the Hague.

But what Charles had perceived only on the scaffold when he dared not, since everything would be overheard, discuss again with Juxon was that, now the people could not listen to his speech, his only way of reaching posterity might be through the printing, by a Royalist press, of that precious paper. That undelivered speech, surely, was what he had so earnestly at the end asked Juxon to 'remember.'

"Having already made my protestations not only against the illegality of this pretended Court," it ran, "but also that no earthly power can justly call me, who am your king, in question as a delinquent; I would not any more open my mouth upon this occasion more than to refer myself to what I have spoken, were I in this case alone concerned. But the duty I owe to God in the preservation of the true liberty of my people will not suffer me at this time to be silent.

"For how can any free-born subject of England call life, or anything that he possesseth, his own, if power without right daily make new, and abrogate the old and fundamental laws of the land; which I now take to be the present case. Wherefore, when I came hither, I expected that you would have endeavoured to have satisfied me concerning these grounds which hinder me to answer to your pretended impeachment. But since I see that nothing I can say will move you to it (though negatives are not so naturally proved as affirmatives) yet I will show you the reason why I am confident you cannot judge me, nor, indeed, the meanest man in England; for I will not (like you), without showing a reason, seek to impose a belief upon my subjects."

At this point the King had written in the margin: "Hereabout I was stopped and not suffered to speak any more concerning reasons."

"There is no proceeding just against any man but what is warranted either by God's laws or the municipal laws of the country where he lives," the manuscript continued. "Now I am most confident this day's proceedings cannot be warranted by God's law, for, on the contrary, the authority of obedience unto kings is clearly warranted and strictly commanded, both in the Old and New Testament, which, if denied, I am ready instantly to prove. And, for the question now in hand, there it is said that: 'Where the word of a King is, there is power, and who may say unto him, "What doest thou?"' (Eccl. viii. 4.)

"Then, of the law of this land, I am no less confident that no learned lawyer will affirm that an impeachment can lie against the King, they all going in his name. And one of their maxims is 'The King can do no wrong.' Besides, the law upon which you ground your proceedings must either be old or new. If old, show it. If new, tell what authority warranted by the fundamental laws of the land hath made it, and when. But how the House of Commons can erect a court of judicature, which was never one itself (as is well known to all lawyers), I leave to God and the world to judge. And it were full strange that they should pretend to make laws without King or Lords' House, to any that have heard speak of the Laws of England.

"And admitting, but not granting, that the people of England's commission could grant your pretended power, I see nothing you can show for that. For certainly you never asked the question of the tenth man in the kingdom. And in this way you manifestly wrong even the poorest ploughman if you demand not his free consent. Nor can you pretend any colour for this your pretended commission without the consent at least of the major part of every man in England, of whatsoever quality or condition, which I am sure you never went about to seek, so far are you from having it.

"Thus you see, I speak not for my own right alone, as I am your King, but also for the true liberty of all my subjects, which consists not in the power of government but in living under such laws, such a government, as may give themselves the best assurance of their lives and the propriety of their goods.

"Nor in this must or do I forget the privileges of both Houses of Parliament which this day's proceedings do not only violate but likewise occasion the greatest breach of their public faith that (I believe) ever was heard of; with which I am far from charging the two Houses, for all the pretended crimes laid against me bear date long before this late Treaty at Newport; in which I, having concluded as much as in me lay and hopefully expecting the Houses' agreement thereunto, was suddenly surprised and hurried from thence as a prisoner. Upon which account I am against my will brought hither; where, since I am come, cannot but to my power defend the ancient laws and liberty of this kingdom, together with my own just right.

"Then, for anything I can see, the Higher House is totally excluded. And, for the House of Commons, it is too well known that the major part of them are detained or deterred from sitting. So, as if I had no other, this were sufficient for me to protest against your pretended court.

"Besides all this, the peace of the Kingdom is not least in my thoughts. And what hope of settlement is there so long as power reigns, without rule of law, changing the whole frame of that government under which this Kingdom hath flourished for many hundred years? Nor will I say what will fall out in case this lawless, unjust proceeding against me do go on. And, believe it, the Commons of England will not thank you for this change, for they will remember how happy they have been of late years under the reign of Queen Elizabeth, the King my father, and myself, until the beginnings of these unhappy troubles; and will have cause to doubt that they shall never be so happy under any new. And, by this time, it will be too sensibly evident that the arms I took up were only to defend the fundamental laws of the kingdom against those who have usurped my power and totally changed the ancient government.

"Thus, having showed you briefly why I cannot submit to your pretended authority without violating the trust I have from God for the welfare and liberty of my people, I expect from you either clear reason to convince my judgment, showing me that I am in error (and then truly I will answer); or that you will withdraw your proceedings."

At the end of it, the King had written: "This I intended to speak in Westminster Hall, on Monday, 22 January, but against reason was hindered."

It was for Juxon to see that it was not hindered for any reason now.

(III) NIGHT

The Four Gentlemen

NOW that the King was dead, his four faithful Gentlemen of the Bedchamber were allowed to attend him privately once more, and when night had fallen, they came back to their master lying embalmed in the Banqueting Hall—the four who, after the King was sentenced, had accused themselves, each individually in his capacity of Privy Councillor, of being alone guilty of what was laid to the King's charge and asked that they might die together in his place; the four who were almost an epitome of the England which had ended that afternoon: James Stuart, fourth Duke of Lennox and first Duke of Richmond; William Seymour, first Marquis and second Earl of Hertford; Montague Bertie, second Earl of Lindsey; and Thomas Wriothesley, fourth Earl of Southampton.

Hertford, who was sixty (he was born in Armada-year), was not only considerably the eldest of them but had played a stranger part than the others in English history. He was of the blood of the Tudor kings and statesmen, for on the distaff side he descended from Henry VII; and on his father's side, he was the great-grandson of the magnificent Protector Somerset[1] who had ruled England in the name of the half-Seymour boy-king Edward VI.

When Sir William Seymour (as Hertford then was) was twenty-one, he had secretly married the Lady Arabella Stuart, who, as King James's first cousin, had been his rival as claimant for the throne of England. The marriage, when it was discovered, threw James into a frenzy of anger and

[1] Charles II, after the Restoration, restored the Dukedom of Somerset to Hertford, with the explanation to Parliament: "If I have done an extraordinary act, it was done for an extraordinary person."

apprehension. On one line of argument, which was never far from the King's mind, Arabella's claim to the English throne was certainly better than his own; for it could be contended that, according to the spirit of the English Constitution, no foreigner could be a lawful king of England and that whereas he was a Scot, born in Scotland, Arabella was an English woman born in England. And, on any theory, her marriage to Seymour, with his inheritance, would make their child too dangerously near the throne on which he precariously sat.

He ordered the immediate arrest and separation of the lovers. Seymour was sent to the Tower and Arabella put under house-arrest at Highgate, as a preliminary to being removed to Durham. By means of friends, the couple communicated with each other and determined to escape from England. A ship was chartered to wait for them in the Thames. On the appointed day, Arabella, having disguised herself as a man "drawing over her petticoats a pair of large French-fashioned hose, putting on a man's doublet, a peruke which covered her hair, a hat, black cloak, russet boots with red tops, and a rapier by her side" managed to elude the vigilance of her keepers and made her way from Highgate to Blackwall where she took a boat, and, with her attendants, was rowed out to the waiting ship, about a mile beyond Lee. But Seymour had not yet arrived, and though Arabella herself would have run all the risks of delay, she was eventually overborne by the fears and importunities of her attendants and allowed the vessel to sail without him.

Seymour, meanwhile, having left his servant in his bed to prevent suspicion, disguised himself in a black wig and a pair of black whiskers and, following a cart that had been directed to bring firewood into his apartment, walked unchallenged out of the Tower, took a boat at Tower Wharf and rowed downstream to the arranged place. When he found that Arabella had sailed without him, he hired another vessel for £40 to take him to Calais where he arrived safely and waited for his wife.

But the disappearance of Arabella from Highgate had soon been discovered and the orders which were immediately sent to the Tower to guard Seymour with increased vigilance led to the discovery of his absence also. King James issued an instant proclamation for their arrest and a fast-sailing vessel which lay in the Downs was ordered to put to sea immediately. The pursuit was successful and though Arabella's pinnace fired thirteen shots before she would strike, she was eventually brought-to. Arabella's only consolation on returning to London, where she was imprisoned in the Tower till her death five years later, was that her husband had escaped.

Seymour remained in Paris until eventually he made his peace with King James, though, under every kind of pressure, he refused to disclose whether or not there was a child of the marriage. Some time after his return to England he married again, this time the sister of the Earl of Essex, who was later to command the Parliamentary Armies in the early stages of the Civil War. He insisted on naming the first child Arabella.

On the death of his grandfather Seymour succeeded to the title as Earl of Hertford when he was thirty-three, and thereupon retired to his country seat in the West, where he lived in great magnificence and became "so wholly given up to country life that he had an aversion, and even an unaptness, for business."

Hertford's experience had given him no particular love for the Stuart dynasty and his second marriage had thrown him among the opponents of the Royal policy. "His greatest acquaintance," according to one who knew him was with "those who had the reputation of being best affected to the liberty of the Kingdom and least in love with the humour of the Court, many of whom were the chief of those who engaged themselves most factiously and furiously against the King." If Charles treated him with slightly more affability than James had done, Hertford had still—in Clarendon's phrase—"received many and continued disobligations from the Court from the time of the King's coming to the crown" and Charles, no less than James, saw to it that "more than ordinary care was taken to discountenance and lessen his interest." Charles, to do him justice, could hardly be unmindful, that, had things fallen out otherwise, Hertford might have been King-Consort of England and he a mere Scottish prince; and history was full of lessons about the peril of over-powerful subjects.

But Hertford did not greatly care. He had had his youth and something more than youth had died in him with Arabella. Also his six years of frustrated exile had made him appreciate to the full his English inheritance, on which he could live *en prince*. Essentially he was a Tudor, living on in a new and unstable age, whose preoccupations and earnestness bored him. He refused even to argue with his guests and friends—"had no delight," as they put it, "in an open and liberal conversation and cared not to discourse or argue on those points which he understood very well, only for the trouble of contending." More and more he turned to his books, for he was a Greek and Latin scholar and had always "loved his book above all exercises." But he was not addicted to theology. He went to church and unenthusiastically supported the Establishment, but no one could have called him pious and it was notorious that he had "no great inclination to the person of any churchman."

When, in 1640, the failure of the Scottish War and the growing political and social discontents were a presage of the troubles to come, Hertford's sympathies naturally did not lie with the Court. He disliked, as much as anyone, the growth of monopolies and the long intermissions of Parliament and, above all, Charles's advisers and the fatuities of their policies. With eleven other peers, he signed a petition against them.

Then, with a flash of insight, he saw where discontent might lead and what hidden fanaticisms lay waiting to control a liberal movement for reform. By blood and training and instinct, he could not do other than stand behind the Crown. Without enthusiasm, he allowed himself to be made a Privy Councillor and he raised a step in the peerage to a Marquisate. He allowed himself, with even less enthusiasm, to be made Governor of the Prince of Wales, "though for the performance of the office of a governor, he never thought himself fit, nor meddled with it." When the Civil War broke out, he found himself accepting from the King the command of the Royal army in the West. The idea of a civil war was so abhorrent to him that he was unable to understand that anyone could really intend to go on with it or even take it seriously and, when the Earl of Bedford with a large army besieged him in Sherborne Castle, he challenged Bedford, who was only twenty-nine, to settle the matter by a personal duel (he was fifty-four at the time). Bedford refused but piously suggested as an alternative that "in godly care to avoid the effusion of Christian blood" he should be allowed to draw off his men from the siege without Hertford firing at them. Hertford retorted that "as they came thither on their own counsels, they should get off as best they could." Both attitudes were typical of him.

Eventually he returned to the King at Oxford where he strove hard for peace, whenever it seemed possible. When the King fled to the Scots, he was left in charge of Oxford and, after his enforced surrender there, made his way to Charles and remained in attendance on him in his journeys and imprisonments as long as he was allowed to.

If Hertford was in the position of an Elizabethan elder statesman, Richmond, the youngest of the four—he was thirty-six—was typical of the *jeunesse dorée* of the reign. As Charles's cousin, he was first in precedence. His father, the third Duke of Lennox, had died when he was twelve, in the last year of the reign of King James. James, as the nearest heir male of the family became, according to Scots custom, his legal tutor and guardian. When Charles came to the throne, he continued the Royal care of the boy; made him Gentleman of the Bedchamber when he was thirteen and Privy Councillor when he was twenty-one. In the interim he was sent on a grand tour of France, Spain and Italy.

At the age of twenty-five, Lennox married the dead Buckingham's only daughter, Mary, whom Charles himself gave away at the splendid wedding. He gave them £20,000 as a wedding-gift and thereafter continued to shower gifts on his young kinsman—land to the value of £3,000 a year; the Keepership of Richmond Park; the Wardenship of the Cinque Ports; and finally the Dukedom of Richmond. He gave him also the exclusive rights of levying dues on the export of raw wool from London—an action which led to trouble with the merchants and increased the nation's anger with the Court when Richmond, with the aid of the navy, impounded all the wool-cargoes at all the ports.

Richmond was a slow young man of no particular ability and, knowing his limitations, was "so diffident of himself that he was sometimes led by men who judged much worse." To an observer in Scotland, where he had been sent by Charles to investigate and report, he made an impression of pure negation—"never declared himself one way or other, never acted anything for the King or against him and was never at any time quarrelled with or questioned by any party."

But this did less than justice to his passionate personal loyalty to his cousin, benefactor and friend. "As he had received great bounties from the King, so he sacrificed all he had to his service, as soon as his occasions stood in need of it," Clarendon left it on record; and Richmond's gifts to Charles of £20,000 on one occasion and £46,000 on another justified the enconium. "He was so punctual in point of honour that he never swerved a tittle. He had so entire a resignation of himself to the King that he abhorred all artifices to shelter himself from the prejudice of those who, how powerful soever, failed in their duty to His Majesty; and therefore he was pursued with all imaginable malice by them, as one that would have no quarter, upon so infamous terms, as but looking on while his master was ill-used."

Lindsey, who was forty, shared the simplicity of Richmond's loyalty but added to it the uncompromising directness of a professional soldier. In his youth, he served in the Low Countries as a cavalry captain and when the Civil War broke out, raised a regiment of horse for the King. At Edgehill, he was taken prisoner, trying to rescue his father, the King's general, who was killed there. In his captivity, he wrote a passionate defence of the Royal cause, which was published under the title of "A Declaration and Vindication of the Earl of Lindsey, now prisoner in Warwick Castle, wherein he makes apparent the justice of His Majesty's cause in taking arms for the preservation of the Royal person and prerogative; as it was sent in a letter to the Right Honourable Henry, Earl of Newark, now resident with His Majesty at Oxford." Eventually he was released in an exchange of prisoners and hurried to the king to fight again at Naseby where he was wounded in command of Charles's life-guard of picked horse.

After the military debâcle, Lindsey was made Gentleman of the Bedchamber and Privy Councillor; and accompanied his master on his travels. In the Isle of Wight, it was, characteristically, Lindsey (supported by Richmond), who had urged Charles to escape from his Army captors while he still had the opportunity. Charles on that occasion—it was two months to the day before his execution—had justified his inaction by treating the desperate situation as if it were a formal diplomatic manœuvre.

"They must preserve me for their own sakes," he had said, "for they cannot secure their own interests without my help as long as my son is out of their reach."

Lindsey had exploded despairingly: "Take heed, sir, lest you fall into their hands. They will not steer by rules of policy. Your escape is your best security."

But even he had not expected his common sense to be justified so soon and so savagely.

The fourth Gentleman, the forty-one-year-old Southampton, was the most remarkable of them, sharply differentiated by his temperament and experience from the rest, though with affinities with them all. He was as forceful as Lindsey, as learned and withdrawn as Hertford and as wealthy as Richmond. The younger son of that Henry Wriothesley who was Shakespeare's early patron (and, some think, the 'W.H.' of the *Sonnets*), he was only fourteen and at Magdalen when his father and his elder brother died together compaigning in the Low Countries, leaving him heir to the vast Wriothesley estates in London and Hampshire—to the seat at Titchfield and vast acres in the New Forest, to the magnificent Southampton House in Holborn and the manor of Bloomsbury. Of a nature predisposed in any case to melancholy, the boy was prostrated by the double death. "He was much troubled to be called 'My Lord' and with the noise of attendance" and retired into himself, delighting only to be alone. As soon as he could, he went abroad and wandered about the Continent for ten years.

On his return, he found that the King had laid claim to a portion of his New Forest property worth £2,000 a year and that the Crown demand had been upheld by a Forest Court; and though Charles, when the young Earl protested in person, generously agreed to forego his claim, Southampton, despite his gratitude, showed no disposition to become one of the Court party or even to fulfil the obligations of etiquette which his station entailed. "He had no relation to, or dependence upon, the Court; or purpose to have any," and "therefore, in the beginning of Parliament, no man was more courted by the Opposition."

During the early days of the political struggle, he took the same line as Hertford (whose seat at Netley was neighbour to his own at Titchfield), protesting against the King's misrule. Like Hertford, he only left the Parliamentary side when he perceived the underlying motives and the logical conclusion of their policy. But, unlike Hertford, he was energetic in debate. "He was a man of great sharpness of judgment, a very quick apprehension and that readiness of expression upon any sudden debate that no man delivered himself more advantageously and weightily and more efficaciously with the hearers; so that no man gave more trouble in his opposition or drew so many to a concurrence with him in opinion."

Yet even when it was quite clear that he must be reckoned among the King's supporters and Charles had offered him the posts of Privy Councillor and Gentleman of the Bed-chamber, Southampton's disdainful individualism for long prevented his acceptance of them and his final concurrence was the result not of Charles's invitation but of Parliament's motion that "no man should be capable of any preferment in Church or State" who dissociated himself from their policy. He immediately accepted the posts to "show how much he contemned those votes."

Once in the King's personal service, his fidelity never wavered, though he outdid even Hertford in his desire for peace and transferred his intransigence to the court circle about the King. At Oxford, just before the flight of the King to the Scots, Southampton had made strictures at the council table which Prince Rupert took as applying to himself. The Prince sent a messenger to expostulate and extort an apology; but Southampton, far from retracting, merely repeated and pointed the language. Rupert thereupon sent a formal challenge to a duel, giving Southampton a choice of weapons. Southampton chose pistols, on the grounds that he was too weak to fight on foot and had no horse to match the Prince's. The duel was arranged for the following morning outside the walls of the city. By this time, however, suspicions had been aroused, "the gates of Oxford were closed to prevent their egress and eventually a reconciliation was effected." Southampton, like the others, left the King only when forced to do so in the November of 1648.

"*Cruel Necessity*"

Of the four Gentlemen, it was Southampton who was watching by the King's body in the Banqueting House that night at the moment when Oliver Cromwell came to look for the last time on the King he had killed.[1]

"The night after King Charles was beheaded my Lord Southampton and a friend of his got leave to sit up by the body in the Banqueting House at Whitehall. As they were sitting very melancholy there about two o'clock in the morning they heard the tread of somebody coming very slowly upstairs. By-and-by the door opened and a man entered very much muffled up in his cloak, and his face quite hid in it. He approached the body, considered it very attentively for some time and then shook his head, sighed out the

[1] Though, of course, the 'friend' mentioned may be one of the other three. It would, indeed, seem likely that they divided the watch between them in pairs.

words 'Cruel necessity.' He then departed in the same slow and concealed manner as he had come. Lord Southampton used to say that he could not distinguish anything of his face; but that by his voice and gait he took him to be Oliver Cromwell."

EPILOGUE TO THE DAY

(1) The Funeral

THE body remained at Whitehall all through the night and the following day, Wednesday, January 31. On that day Juxon, who had been further cross-examined about the meaning of 'Remember' without in any way adding to or altering his original explanation, was at last discharged from arrest; and, in the Commons, Ireton had his revenge by proposing and carrying that "a paper of divers particulars concerning the late King's body, his George, his diamond and two seals" should not be sent to the Prince of Wales.

On the Wednesday night under cover of darkness to circumvent any danger of a popular demonstration of sympathy, Charles's body was taken back to St. James's and there for some days lay exposed to public view—so that any sceptic, provided an admission fee were paid, could convince himself that the King was indeed dead.

As Cromwell had still given no orders for a burial, Herbert and Juxon discussed where they should, were they allowed, inter their master. To neither of them had Charles expressed any preference nor had they considered it "in his lifetime a proper question for either of them to ask, albeit they had oftentimes the opportunity." Eventually they decided to ask for permission to bury their King in Westminster Abbey. "They thought no place more fit to inter the corpse than in King Henry VII's Chapel at the east end of Westminster Abbey" where Charles's brother Henry and his father James and his grandmother, Mary Queen of Scots, all lay.

It might have been taken for granted that permission would be denied, though neither Juxon nor Herbert had anticipated the unexpected honesty of the reason which accompanied Parliament's refusal—"that probably it would attract infinite numbers of people of all sorts thither to see where the King was buried, which (as the times then were) was judged unsafe and inconvenient."

Herbert and Juxon then made their second choice. "They then resolved to bury the King's body in the Royal Chapel of St. George within the castle of Windsor, both in regard His Majesty was Sovereign of the Most Noble Order of the Garter: and that several kings, his ancestors, are there interred, namely, King Henry VI, King Edward IV and King Henry VIII. It was also a castle and place His Majesty took great delight in, as in discourse he oft times expressed. Upon which considerations, Mr. Herbert made his second address to the Committee of Parliament who, after some deliberation, gave him an order bearing date the 6th of February."

Parliament, stipulating that the whole expense of the funeral was not to exceed £500, appointed in charge of the proceedings, in addition to Herbert, three men who had for the last three years been, like him loyal to them and personally friendly to Charles—Captain Antony Mildmay, Major Thomas Duckett and Captain Robert Preston. Of the four, three had been appointed, a year ago, at Carisbrooke to be in perpetual attendance on Charles in the following terms: "Four Gentlemen of approved integrity, Mr. Herbert, Mr. Mildmay, Captain Titus and Captain Preston, constantly to attend the person of the King in their courses by two at a time, who are to be always in his presence, except when he retires into his bedchamber and then they are to repair the one to one door and the other to the other, and there to continue until the King comes forth again."

Titus, however, had not proved worthy of the trust. He had gone over to the King, tried to engineer his escape from Carisbrooke and managing to evade arrest was now in the service of Charles II in France. Major Duckett, who had replaced Titus, had also been removed from the King's service before the trial, but he was allowed to return for this last office. He had been the Gentleman Sewer in the Royal Household as it was established in captivity, as Preston had been Gentleman of the Robes, Mildmay Gentleman Carver and Herbert Gentleman of the Bedchamber.

To these four was entrusted the order to bury the King where they thought fit in either the Choir or Chapel at Windsor; and to the four faithful Royalist Gentlemen of the Bedchamber—Richmond, Hertford, Lindsey and Southampton—permission was given, as it was to Juxon, to attend the ceremony. In addition, Richmond, who was known to be Charles's executor in this matter, was given the right, if he chose to attend, to bury the King in whatever part of the Royal Chapel he wished.

On Friday, February 9, the cortège set out from St. James's Palace for Windsor. The King's body "was carried in a hearse covered with black velvet, drawn by six horses also covered with black. Four coaches followed, two of them covered likewise with black cloth, in which were about two dozen Gentlemen and others, most of them being such as had waited on His Majesty at Carisbrooke Castle and other places." Murry, the King's coachman, drove the hearse.

When they arrived at Windsor, Herbert showed Colonel Whichcote, the Governor of the Castle, their authorization and the coffin was taken to the King's usual bedroom there, while the Dean's Hall was prepared for its reception. The room was hung with black, on walls and over the windows, by Richard Harrison and lighted by three dozen torches which had been supplied by faithful John Joyner, the Master Cook, who was the only servant except Herbert to be with Charles from the beginning of his captivity to the end of it. When all was considered seemly the coffin was brought down and laid on the table in the centre of the Hall.

Herbert, Mildmay, Duckett and Preston then went across to St. George's Chapel "to take a view thereof and of the most fit and honourable place for the Royal corpse to rest in."

At first, they thought that the Tomb-House, which had been built by Cardinal Wolsey as a monument to Henry VIII, would be the most suitable place. Henry VIII was supposed to be buried there—though no one knew certainly where his grave was, except that it was somewhere at Windsor—and Herbert objected that Charles had been no admirer of that King, since "His Majesty (who was a real Defender of the Faith and as far from censuring any as might be) would upon occasional discourse express some dislike of King Harry's proceedings in misemploying those vast revenues the suppressed abbeys, monasteries and other religious houses were endowed with, and by demolishing those many stately structures which might at the Reformation have in some measure been kept up and converted to sundry pious uses." If this argument were not strong enough to disallow any proximity to Henry VIII—though no one was inclined to dispute it—an overwhelming case against the selection of Wolsey's mausoleum was that, as it only adjoined the Chapel Royal and was not actually inside it, it did not conform with the terms of the order.

The four "next pitched upon the vault where King Edward IV is interred, being in the north side of the choir, near the altar under a fair large stone of tuke, raised within the opposite arch, having a range of iron bars gilt, curiously cut according to Church work." Herbert remembered that Charles was an admirer of the Yorkist king 'from whom His Majesty was lineally propagated,' and orders were given to have the vault opened.

The work had hardly been started, however, when Juxon, accompanied by Richmond, Hertford, Lindsey and Southampton, who had travelled direct to Windsor, came into the

Chapel. Herbert immediately deferred to their choice of the place of burial. Like Herbert, though for the topographical rather than the theological reasons, they rejected the Tomb-House, but were unable to make a positive choice until one of them "beating gently upon the pavement with his staff perceived a hollow sound and, ordering the stones and earth thereunder to be removed, discovered a descent into a vault where two coffins were laid near one another—the one very large and of antique form; the other, little." They decided, though there was no distinguishing mark, that these were the coffins of Henry VIII and his third wife, Jane Seymour, mother of King Edward VI, an identification, Herbert recorded, which "may be credited, for as Mr. Brook, York-Herauld, in his catalogue of the nobility, p. 40, observes, no other of King Harry's six wives was buried at Windsor." The velvet palls over them still appeared fresh "albeit laid there 130 years and upwards."

The Lords, who either did not know or did not respect, Charles's antipathy to 'King Harry' ordered "that the King's body should there be interred (being about the middle of the choir over against the eleventh stall upon the sovereign's side)." Hertford, indeed, might even be said to have an interest in having Charles buried with his great-aunt, Jane. But the discussions about possible identification had made them determine that there should be no such doubts about the present burial and they sent workmen back to the Hall to cut in lead the King's name and the year: "King Charles, 1648."[1]

The workmen went back to the Dean's Hall to carry this out and had not returned by the time that Richmond and his companions left the Chapel. They "gave the sexton order to lock the Chapel door, not suffering any to stay till further notice. The sexton did his best to clear the chapel; neverthe-

[1] In England the Julian calendar was still followed and the years were reckoned as beginning on Lady Day.

less (he said) a foot-soldier had hid himself so as was not discerned, and, being greedy of prey, got into the vault and cut so much of the velvet pall as he judged would hardly be missed and wimbled a hole into the coffin that was the largest, probably fancying there was something well worth his adventure. The sexton, at his opening the door, espied the sacrilegious person, who being searched a bone was also found about him which, he said, he would haft a knife with. The Governor gave him his reward."

"This manifests," adds Herbert in his account, "that a real body was there; which some, that have hard thoughts of King Harry, have scrupled."

As soon as the workmen had returned and both coffin and grave were ready, the funeral procession from the Hall to the Chapel started at "a slow and solemn pace, (much sorrow in most faces discernable)." The coffin was carried by soldiers, but over it was a black velvet pall held up like a canopy by Richmond, Hertford, Lindsey and Southampton at each corner. The King's servants who had been with him in his imprisonment went first before it, with Herbert and his three companions nearest the coffin, followed immediately by Juxon and Colonel Whichcote, the Governor. When the body was set down by the bearers near the grave, Richmond asked that Juxon might use the service for the Burial of the Dead from the Book of Common Prayer. Whichcote, however, felt that he could not allow this, because the use of the Book was illegal, though he explained that Juxon could use what extempore prayer he liked. The Bishop, still mindful of Charles's likes and dislikes, preferred not and "the King's body was laid in the vault without any words or other ceremonies than the tears and the sighs of the few beholders."

But there was one particular circumstance which Herbert thought worth recording. "This is memorable," he wrote, "that at such time as the King's body was brought out of St.

George's Hall the sky was serene and clear; but immediately it began to snow, and fell so fast as by that time they came to the west end of the Royal Chapel the black velvet pall was all white, the colour of innocency. So went the White King to his grave."

(ii) The Killing of the Regicides

"I WENT to Charing Cross to see Major-General Harrison hanged, drawn and quartered," recorded Samuel Pepys on October 13, 1660. "Thus it was my chance to see the King beheaded at White Hall, and to see the first blood shed in revenge for the King at Charing Cross."

Thus Mr. Pepys accomplished a perspective which posterity is apt to ignore. To consider the day they killed the King in isolation is to see it falsely, with the scales intolerably weighted in Charles's favour. Also, it is to reduce tragedy to pity without terror.

The balance has been well defined by an historian of Puritanism who, in a memorable passage uses the word 'sacrament' in its original sense of a military oath: "In the presence of death, the King recovered all his dignity, and fell back upon his noblest line of defence—his loyalty to the form of religion in which he had been nurtured. He was no longer driven by fate to conciliate Presbytery or coquet with Catholicism. With the end of intrigue and duplicity came the opportunity for sincerity. The long day of craft and falsehood was about to close, and the one clear faith which Charles had never wholly forsworn, though he had cruelly compromised it, came back to be his support at the last. How bravely and royally he bore himself in that final scene at Whitehall we all know. Yet not less admirable than the bearing of Charles was the stern determination of his rugged conquerors that even by the blood of so illustrious a victim, and the consequent horror and consternation of the world, the rights of Englishmen should be vindicated and the liberties of religion guaranteed. For this they had fought and prayed and suffered, and on that scaffold at Whitehall, on that frosty morning of 30 January 1649, their 'sacrament' was kept."

The days were to come when those victors, too, had to pay for their beliefs in blood; to submit to trials equally illegal and to deaths far more horrible in an atmosphere of popular blood-lust and hatred. And they paid with such courage and steadfastness that the crowds, which at the beginning were comparable with the decadents yelling for death in a Roman circus, at the end forced the Royalist Government to abandon its vengeance.

October 13, 1660, and the days which followed are more than a sequel to January 30, 1649. They are an important part of the same picture. To see Colonel Daniel Axtell, for instance, only in the guise we have so far seen him is to mis-estimate the man. Every history book records the episode of his calling out for vengeance on Charles at the trial; but few, if any, recall his own end—his repudiation, as scornful as Charles's, of the right of the Court to sentence him: his remark as he lay in prison after sentence, to a friend who was going abroad: "Sir, pray remember my love to all my Christian friends there and tell them that you saw me in my chains; and tell them that, for that Good Old Cause which we were engaged in, I am now going to be their martyr. And as for the King, I wish him as well as my own soul. But they have merely murdered me and they might as well have done it at the Tower as brought me hither to make this bustle. They had nothing in God's law or their own to condemn me, but it was enough my name was Axtell." To another friend, who asked for a message for acquaintances in Gloucestershire, he said: "Bid them, whatever they do, love the image of Christ wherever they see it, in presbyterian, independent, baptized or other; and take heed of striking in with anything that will strike any out of the offices of Jesus Christ." He cheered his fellow-prisoner with: "Well, our God is the God of Newgate, too": described the ladder at the gibbet as 'a Jacob's ladder,' and, as he went to death, 'calling for his Bible, he hugged it saying: "This hath the whole Cause in it and I may carry it without offence." '

And there was Carew, taunted as he went to execution by the Royalist crowd: "This is the rogue who will have no king but Jesus," affirming on the one hand his religious faith as they laid him on the hurdle: "My Lord Jesus for the joy that was set before him endured the cross and despised the shame; whose steps I desire to follow" and, on the other not at all abating his republicanism: spoke of "the way they are taking to destroy us who did not think the King's person sacred" and hoped that "our blood will make many hundreds more persuaded of the truth of it." And Thomas Scot who, being refused permission to speak to the people from the scaffold, contented himself with: "It must be a very mean and bad cause which cannot bear the words of a dying man." And John Jones welcoming the hurdle with: "This is like Elijah's fiery chariot, only it goes through Fleet Street." And Adrian Scroop who, while waiting to be taken to his agony, said to his companion in the cell: "Do you spend your time as the Lord shall direct you. I intend to take a little sleep, for I slept not well last night; and my countenance is not so fresh as I would have it." 'Thereupon he laid him down and slept so soundly that he snored very loud and so continued till the sled came for him; whereupon, being awakened, he riseth up; and a friend taking him in his arms and asking him how he did? he answers, Very well, I thank God, never better in all my life. And now, saith he, will I wash my hands in innocency, so will I compass thine altar, O Lord: and so with great cheerfulness went to execution.' And Okey, *par excellence* the fighting-man, who had defied Cromwell as well as Charles, taking a piece of straw, and saying "I do no more value what I am now going about than this. I have made many a charge in my time; but now I have but one charge to make and then I shall be at rest," and bore himself so that the executioners remarked that 'he was as lusty, stout, brave a man as ever fought in England.'

It was Okey's execution which made any more impossible. Since he had been tried not for high treason or for killing the King but merely for the 'felony' of having fled to Holland (where he was betrayed by the English agent), his body was allowed to his wife to be buried. She decided that he should lie in his family vault in Christ Church, Stepney; and when the news spread, no less than twenty thousand people surged to Stepney to pay their last respects to him. So alarmed were the Government by this demonstration that the order was promptly revoked and Okey hurried to an unknown grave in the Tower, "having," it was said, "written his epitaph in the hearts of the people."

Not all the regicides were consoled by their religious convictions. Henry Marten had the detachment of the fatalistic stoicism he professed. His epitaph, which he composed in the form of an acrostic, revealed the man:

H ere or elsewhere (all's one to you, to me)
E arth, air or water grips my ghostless dust
N one knows how soon to be by fire set free,
R eader, if you an oft-tried rule will trust,
Y ou'll gladly do and suffer what you must.

M y life was spent in serving you, and you,
A nd death's my pay, it seems: and welcome too;
R evenge destroying but itself, while I
T o birds of prey leave my old cage, and fly.
E xamples preach to th'eye. Care then (mine says)
N ot how you end, but how you spend your days.

As it happened, he escaped with his life to spend twenty years in prison. As an old man, he was asked whether, if the scene could be brought back and the actors introduced again on the stage of life, he would sign the warrant for the death of his sovereign. As 'all that he moved for was on Roman or Greek principles,' the impenitent republican instantly replied in the affirmative.

The King's last leave-taking of his family is, rightly, part of the story of England. But, in this respect, Death is indeed a leveller and the regicides, too, had wives and children. Though their story is forgotten, it is not less memorable—John Cook's last comforting of his weeping wife: "My dear lamb, why weepest thou? Let them weep who part and shall never meet again; but I am confident we shall have a glorious meeting in Heaven. Here our comforts have been mixed with chequer-work of troubles, but in Heaven all tears shall be wiped from our eyes": John Jones, whose family was not present, trying to console Colonel Scroop's children: "You are weeping for your father, but suppose your father were to-morrow to be the King of France and you were to tarry a little behind, would you weep so? Why, he is going to the King of Kings and everlasting glory"; and, on the scaffold, seeing his enemies in terms of humanity: "I must confess I very freely quit His Majesty, considering what he hath done in this case is the part of a loving son to a father, especially with the judges telling him it is the law": Barkstead, when his hurdle was passing the window at which his wife was standing, taking off his hat and waving it at her with the apology: "To Heaven, to Heaven, my love, and leave you in the storm": and Miles Corbet, whose wife was beside herself with grief, trying to steady her by a familiar family joke and 'though tears were ready to start from his eyes, yet he conquered himself, and taking his wife by the hand, said: O, my dear wife, shall we part in a shower? (which words he had used before) God will be a husband and a father to thee and thine; and so, kissing her, turned to his son Miles, whom he took by the hand and blessed him also; and then hastened to the sledge, desiring a friend to stay by his wife and his son, to comfort them.'

When the Government found it too dangerous to indulge in further executions, they turned their energies to the dead. The wax effigy of Oliver Cromwell which, like those of other rulers of England, had been deposited in Westminster Abbey, was exhibited to the public at the Jewel House at Whitehall, hanging from a window-bar with a rope round its neck. Cromwell's body, with those of Ireton and Bradshawe, was dug up, drawn through the streets on hurdles, hanged up at Tyburn and then buried under the gallows. The heads were severed from their trunks and exhibited on pikes in Westminster Hall.

Even Mr. Pepys thought this not altogether worthy when he recorded the proceeding "which (methinks) do trouble me that a man of so great courage as he was should have that dishonour, though otherwise he might deserve it enough."[1] But the Government was insatiable. The bodies of Elizabeth Cromwell, Oliver's mother, and Elizabeth Claypole, his favourite daughter; of Robert Blake, the famous admiral, who after his victory at Santa Cruz died in Plymouth Sound, having his last prayer, that he might at

[1] The Government had originally intended to re-inter the body of Charles I with as much pomp and splendour as could be compassed, but the state of public opinion made it too dangerous and it was given out that the King's body could not be found. Cromwell, it was said, had moved the bodies of various sovereigns and there was no certainty about the locality of the King's corpse. It was also suggested that, after Cromwell's death, his friends, anticipating that, in a Royalist reaction, some indignity might be offered to his dead body had moved the King's body from St. George's Chapel at Windsor and placed it in Cromwell's coffin in Westminster Abbey, having first removed the Protector's body and buried it on the battlefield of Naseby. This story gained more credence among the people because of the hurried way in which the proceedings at Tyburn were conducted and the comparatively little time people had to recognize the head and face of the Protector; and the Puritans, naturally, took full advantage of this to spread the story that the Royalists, while they thought they were desecrating the bones of Oliver, were in fact dishonouring Charles by burying him beneath the common gallows. This absurd tale persisted through the centuries and was not finally disposed of until, in 1813, George IV, then Prince of Wales, ordered Charles's grave in St. George's Chapel to be re-opened and the corpse examined.

least see England once more, granted; of John Pym and William Stroud, two of the 'Five Members' whom Charles infringed the rights of the Commons to arrest; of Thomas May, who wrote the *History of the Long Parliament*, and of Sir William Constable, Governor of Gloucester and a regicide; of several Cromwellian colonels and Presbyterian divines—all these were disinterred and "with some others of lesser note, both men and women were thrown together in one pit . . . but the work was so indecent and carried with it such popular odium that a stop was put to any further proceedings."

It is easy enough to moralize on the subject in the light of subsequent happenings. And, indeed, the insult to Blake and Deane (who fought under him when he engaged Van Tromp in the Channel and wrested the supremacy of the seas from Holland for England), has supplied a text to one historian: "Their ashes were avenged when, in 1667, their old enemy the Dutch sailed unmolested up the Thames, burnt the *Royal James* and the British fleet off their own dockyard at Chatham, captured the *Royal Charles*, and, emptying it of its guns and ammunition, towed it down the Channel under the ill-served guns of Upnor Castle and to the amazement and shame of a thousand spectators. Then did people sigh for one day of the Protector and cry out for Fairfax the Independent, and Ingoldsby the regicide and other Puritan survivors of Cromwell's commanders, to wipe away the disgrace that the Stuart had brought upon the country. And then did the court and the court caterpillars quake with fear lest it should get to the ears of the people and of Parliament . . . that the Royal admirals in their abject terror and bewilderment had sunk one of their own ships loaded with stores and ammunition for the fleet and another of the French king's laden with £80,000 worth of cargo in mistake for the enemy. And many an old Ironside and many an old salt, must have turned from the sight of the British fleet in flames, without their officers having fired a gun or drawn a sword, and sworn how different things would have been were Blake at Chatham or Deane at Sheerness."

Yet it is not by subsequent fortuities, impressive though they may appear, that the situation can be judged. Integrity must be set against integrity, trial against trial, death against death, to give true perspective to the day they killed the King. And in the proceedings against Thomas Harrison who was the first of the regicides to be proceeded against, the balancing factor can be found.

Harrison was chosen to be the first because his case was thought to be the strongest. He was an impenitent 'Leveller'; owning only 'the Kingdom of Christ', he had openly opposed the King and advocated his death; he had alienated many of his own party by defying Cromwell when the Protector forsook his republican principles; and he was believed by the Royalists to have been unmannerly and vindictive to Charles. On the other hand, the strength of his convictions and his soldierly fortitude were such that there was little likelihood of his recantation.

At the time of his trial, Harrison was fifty-four. He came of a landed family in Durham (whom he eventually alienated by his political views). He was an M.A. of Oxford University, from which he proceeded to the Inns of Court and as a young barrister he had enlisted in Essex's bodyguard at the very outset of the Civil War. He had fought all through it—at Marston Moor and at Naseby, at Preston and at Worcester. As a cavalry Colonel, his regiment, unquestionably one of the bravest in the army, was composed almost exclusively of religious enthusiasts and held prayer-meetings at halts on their march. During Cromwell's absence in Scotland, Harrison was appointed as Commander-in-Chief in England. He had sat as M.P. for Wendover since 1646, but was active in the expulsion of the Long Parliament and a leading spirit in 'Barebone's Parliament.' Of his sons, one had already emigrated to Virginia[1] and the other was, at the time of the trial, in Vienna and so escaped the Royalist vengeance.

If the tribunal which tried the King was packed with his enemies, so was Harrison's. Indeed the composition of the Commission appointed to try the regicides was, in one sense, even more heavily weighted against the prisoners, since to fanatical royalists were added renegade Cromwellians, each ultimately as guilty on the same charge as the men they were trying. The President was Sir Orlando Bridgeman who had not only acknowledged Cromwell but, with his assent, practised in the courts under what he now called the 'usurpation'; Monck, Oliver's trusted subordinate, had occupied the same position in Scotland—Commander-in-Chief—as Harrison had occupied in England: Denzil Holles and Lord Manchester were two of the 'Five Members' who had been mainly instrumental in raising the first army against the King; Arthur Annesley, who belonged to the same group and had fought against the King in Ireland, was not only a Commissioner, but chose to address the jury against Harrison. "These men," as one legal historian has it, "after the fashion of perverts, to show their loyalty to the rising sun, set themselves with the utmost diligence to destroy all those who had with themselves been worshippers of the sun that had set."[2]

The grand jury met at Hickes's Hall in St. John's Street, Clerkenwell, which was used as a Court of Petty Session, on October 9, 1660, and the bills then found were sent for trial at the October Sessions of the Old Bailey on the following day.

CLERK: Thomas Harrison, how sayest thou? Art thou guilty of the Treason whereof thou standest indicated and art now arraigned? Or Not Guilty?

[1] From him was descended William Henry Harrison, eighth President of the United States.

[2] F. A. Inderwick, Q.C., in his essay, "The Regicides" in *Side-Lights on the Stuarts*.

HARRISON: My lords, have I liberty to speak?

CLERK: No more, at this time, than Guilty or Not Guilty.

HARRISON: Will you give me leave to give you my answer in my own words?

BRIDGEMAN: There is no answer but what the law directs; it is the same with you as with all others, or as I would desire if I were in your condition. You must plead Not Guilty or, if you confess Guilty, there must be judgment upon your confession.

HARRISON: You express your rule very fairly, but I have something to say to Your Lordships which concerns Your Lordships as well as myself.

BRIDGEMAN: You must hold and plead Guilty or Not Guilty.

HARRISON: My lord, I have been kept close prisoner near these three months, that nobody might have access to me. Do you call me to give a legal answer, not knowing of my trial till nine o'clock last night, and brought away from the tower to this place at six o'clock this morning?

BRIDGEMAN: You must give your direct answer. Guilty or Not Guilty. You cannot say it is sudden or unprovided. You spend time in vain. You trouble the Court. You must plead Guilty or Not Guilty. We will not suffer you to make discourses here. You must plead either Guilty or Not Guilty.

SOLICITOR-GENERAL: I beseech your lordships he may plead; peradventure he knows his case so well that he thinks it as cheap to defy the Court as submit to it.

HARRISON: Will you give me your advice?

BRIDGEMAN: We do give you advice. The advice is that there is no other plea than Guilty or Not Guilty.

HARRISON: You do deny me counsel, then I do plead Not Guilty.

CLERK: How will you be tried?

HARRISON: I will be tried according to the laws of the Lord.

BRIDGEMAN: Now I must tell you, if you do not answer 'By God and the Country' you have said nothing.

CLERK: How will you be tried? Will you put yourself on God and the Country?

HARRISON: I put myself upon what you please to put me upon.

BRIDGEMAN: You are versed in the proceedings of the law. You know quite well that you must put yourself upon the trial of God and your Country. If you do not, it was as if you had said nothing. We must record your standing mute.

CLERK: How will you be tried?

HARRISON: I will be tried according to the ordinary course.

CLERK: 'By God and the Country.' You must speak the words.

HARRISON: They are vain words.

BRIDGEMAN: We have given you a great deal of liberty and scope, which is not usual. It is the course and proceedings of law that you must put yourself of God and your Country.

CLERK: How will you be tried?

HARRISON: I offer myself to be tried in your own way—by God and my Country.

CLERK: God send you a good deliverance.

The reason for Harrison's dilemma was made clear the next day when he came to trial at the Old Bailey. 'Guilty' or 'Not Guilty' as an alternative in this case did not at all cover the actuality of the situation. He had not the least intention of denying what he had done, but, since he had done it under authority, it was impossible to plead 'Guilty.' When, on October 11, witness after witness was called to establish what had never been in doubt—that Harrison had been one of the King's judges and had signed the death-warrant—he accepted it as a matter of course with "I do not wish to deny anything that in my own judgment and conscience I have done or committed, but I want rather to bring it into the light." And he explained, in passing, his objection to the theory that he would be tried by 'his country' when, in reply to his opponents' "Your countrymen will cry out and shame you," he answered quietly: "May be so, my lords. Some will, but I am sure others will not." The court which tried Harrison was no more representative of the people of England than was the court which had tried Charles, and the phrase 'by the Country' was indeed nothing but "vain words."

The opening of his defence showed how little he was concerned to deny his action, however strongly he might repudiate personal 'guilt.'

HARRISON: My lords, the matter that hath been offered to you was not a thing done in a corner. I believe the sound of it hath been in most nations. I believe the hearts of some have felt the terrors of that presence of God that was with His servants in those days (however it seemeth good to Him to suffer this turn to come upon us) and are witnesses that the things were not done in a corner.

For myself, I do profess that I would not offer of myself the least injury to the poorest man or woman that goes upon the earth. I humbly submit this to your Lordships: You know as well as I what a contest there has been in these nations for many years. Some of those that now sit on the Bench were at one time as active——

This sudden intrusion of fact and reality was what the Bench had most feared. Bridgeman cut him short.

BRIDGEMAN: Pray, Mr. Harrison, do not cast reflections on the Court. That is not the business in hand.

But Harrison was determined to make his point and with growing uneasiness his judges listened.

HARRISON: I did not follow my own judgment. I did what I did as out of conscience to the Lord. Rather than turn, as many did that set their hands to this plough, I chose rather to be separated from my wife and family than to have compliance with them, though they said 'Sit at my right-hand' and such kind expressions. Thus I have given a little poor testimony that I have not been doing things for myself. May be I might be a little mistaken; but I did it all according to the best of my understanding.

I humbly conceive that what was done was done in the name of the Parliament of England; was done by their power and authority; and I humbly submit that neither this Court nor any court less than Parliament itself has jurisdiction over their actions. What was done was done by the authority of the Parliament, which was then the Supreme Authority; and those who acted under them cannot be questioned by any inferior power. According to the laws of nations, that was a due Parliament. Our Commissions were issued by them and what was done was done by their power; and whereas it has been said that we assumed and usurped an authority, I say that we acted in the fear of the Lord.

During this speech, the Bench had become increasingly restive and, as he paused, Bridgeman burst out savagely:

BRIDGEMAN: Away with him. Do you know where you are, sir? You are in the assembly of Christians. Will you make God the author of your treasons and murders? We will allow you to say for your own defence what you can; and we have with a great deal of patience suffered you to sally out, wherein you have not gone about so much for extenuation of your crimes as to justify them, to fall upon others, to blaspheme God and to commit a new treason.

SOLICITOR-GENERAL: Though my Lords here have been pleased to give you a great latitude, you must not be allowed to run into these damnable excursions, to make God the author of these damnable treasons committed.

HARRISON: I have two things to say in my defence as a matter of law. One is that this that hath been done was done by a Parliament of England, by the Commons of England assembled in Parliament; and, that being so, whatever was done by their commands or their authority is not questionable by your Lordships, as being (as I humbly conceive) a power inferior to that of the High Court of Parliament. That is one. The second is this—that what anyone did in obedience to that power and authority cannot be questioned for it; otherwise we are in a most miserable condition, bound to obey those in authority and yet punished if we do obey.

SOLICITOR-GENERAL: These two points, my lords, are but one and they are a new treason, at the bar, for which he deserves to die, even if there were no other indictment. It is the malice of his heart to the dignity and crown of England. The Lords and Commons are not a Parliament; the Lords and Commons cannot do anything without the King, especially against the King. If they do, they must answer it with their head; for the King is not accountable to any coercive power.

BRIDGEMAN: It is true. Your questions are but one point. You pretend to Parliament's authority and yet, when you come to speak of it, you say the Commons of England. I would fain know of you wherever you read, by the light you say you have in your conscience, that the Commons of England were a Parliament of England? He hath a great deal of charity who thinks that what you did was from a conscientious principle; it was against the light of noon-day and common practice. You make yourself a Solicitor in the business: 'Let us blacken him as much as we can.' You justify it upon 'convictions of conscience' and pretend it upon authority; a thing never known or seen under the sun, that the Commons, nay a few Commons alone, should take upon them and call themselves the Parliament of England. We have been cheated enough by names and words. There is no colour for what you say.

Technically, what Bridgeman said was true enough. In fact, as everyone there knew, it was nonsense. As Axtell was later to point out, the Parliament was called into being by the King before the outbreak of the Civil War and had never dissolved, though its composition was changed. It was from this authority that Manchester himself had obtained his commission when he was appointed Commander: it was this authority which commissioned Monck: it was this authority which was recognized by the other nations of Europe, who sent their ambassadors to Oliver. It had been the only effective authority for the last eighteen years and to question it was to question the validity of every legal, constitutional and international act for almost a generation. Men like Bridgeman and Annesley and Hollis had obeyed it and now they, as well as several of the judges, united in denying it. To the ensuing spate of 'constitutional' eloquence, Harrison replied:

HARRISON: Notwithstanding the judgment of so many learned ones that the Kings of England are in no way accountable to the Parliament, the Lords and Commons, in the beginning of this way, having declared the King's beginning war upon them, the God of Gods——

BRIDGEMAN: Do you render yourself so desperate that you care not what language you let fall? It must not be suffered.

HARRISON: I would not willingly speak to offend any man. The King's setting up his standard against the people——

BRIDGEMAN: Truly, Mr. Harrison, this must not be suffered: this doth not at all belong to you.

HARRISON: Under favour, this doth belong to me. I would have abhorred to have brought him to account, had not the blood of Englishmen that had been shed——

A LAWYER: Methinks he should be sent to Bedlam till he comes to the gallows to render an account of this. It is in a manner an impeachment of *this* king, to justify their treasons against his late Majesty.

SIR EDWARD TURNER: My lords, this man hath the plague all over him. It is a pity that any should stand near him, for he will infect them. Let us say to him what they used to write over an infected house: 'The Lord have mercy upon him,' and so let the officer take him away.

BRIDGEMAN: Mr. Harrison, we are ready to hear you again; but to hear such stuff, it cannot be suffered. You have spoken that which is as high a degree of blasphemy (next to that against God) as I have heard. To extenuate your crimes you may go on; but you must not go on as before.

HARRISON: I must not speak so as to be pleasing to men; but if I am not allowed to have the liberty of an Englishman——

A JUDGE: Pray do not reflect on the Court in that fashion. You have had more liberty than any prisoner in your condition can expect. I wish you had made good use of it. If you keep to the business, you can say what you will.

HARRISON: Then, my lords, thus. One of the witnesses said that I was at the Committee preparing the Charge against the King and that I said: "Let us blacken him." This is utterly untrue. I abhorred the doing of anything to blacken the King. There was a little discourse between the King and myself. The King had told me that he had heard that I should come privately to the Isle of Wight to offer some injury to him; but I told him that I abhorred the thoughts of it. And whereas it is said that my conduct was hard to him when I brought him to London, it was not I who brought him to London. I was commanded by the General to fetch him from Hurst Castle. I do not remember any hard conduct towards him.

BRIDGEMAN: If you have nothing more to say which tends to your justification, we must direct the jury. The purpose of your speeches is merely to infect the people.

HARRISON: You are uncharitable in that.

A JUDGE: My lords, this ought not to come from the Bar to the Bench. If you have anything to say by way of excuse for yourself as matter of fact, you may speak; but if you go as you have been doing, you will not be suffered.

HARRISON: The things that have been done upon the stage in the sight of the sun——

A JUDGE: All this is a continuance of the justification and a confession of the fact.

COUNSEL: He hath confessed the fact, my lords. The matter itself is treason upon treason; and therefore we pray direction to the jury.

BRIDGEMAN: Mr. Harrison, I must give direction to the jury if you will not go further touching the fact.

HARRISON: My lords, I say that what I did was by the Supreme Authority; I have said it before and appeal to your consciences that this Court cannot call me in question.

BRIDGEMAN: Mr. Harrison, you have appealed to our consciences. We shall do what is just, for which we shall answer before the Tribunal of God. Pray take heed of an obdurate, hard heart and a scarred conscience.

HARRISON: My lords, I have been kept six months a close prisoner and could not prepare myself for this trial by counsel. I have got here some Acts of Parliament of that House of Commons which your Lordship will not own and their proceedings whose authority I do own.

BRIDGEMAN: If you show never so many of that nature, they will not help you.

Bridgeman then gave his charge to the jury, in which, since Harrison had admitted that he was one of those guilty of 'compassing, imagining and contriving the death of our late sovereign Lord, King Charles the First, of blessed memory' there was little to do except re-emphasize the fact. "He hath been so far from denying that he hath justified these actions," said the Lord Chief Baron. "I think you need not go out." The jury immediately and unanimously brought in the verdict of 'Guilty' and after Harrison had said: "I have nothing further to say, because the Court has not seen fit to listen. I submit to the judgment," Bridgeman pronounced the death-sentence:

BRIDGEMAN: The judgment of the Court is that you be led back to the place whence you came, and from thence to be drawn on an hurdle to the place of execution; and there you shall be hanged by the neck and, while still alive, shall be cut down and your privy members cut off, your entrails taken out of your body and, you living, the same to be burnt before your eyes, and your head to be cut off, your body to be divided into four quarters, and head and quarters to be disposed of at the pleasure of the King's Majesty. And may the Lord have mercy on your soul.

As soon as the sentence had been pronounced, Harrison said: "Whom men have judged, God doth not condemn. Blessed be the name of the Lord," He was taken back to Newgate with the crowd surging round him, shouting in triumph and derision; but he answered them: 'Good is the Lord for all this. I have no reason to be ashamed of the cause I have been engaged in." But there were some friends there too and to them he explained, as they pressed near him, "I could not be better if I had been granted my heart's desire. We must be willing to receive hard things from our Father as well as easy things."

During his trial, in conformity with principle that no man may be tried in chains, the irons which worn for so many months, had eaten their way into his wrists and ankles, had been struck off. Now, as he returned to his dark cell, the gaoler stood ready to rivet them on again. Though Harrison had but one more night to spend—since the Court, deciding to press their advantage to the utmost, had decreed his immediate death in the morning—he must spend it in discomfort. As the chains were put on his ankles, he said: "This is nothing, compared with what Christ suffered for me."

The woman who cleaned his cell was still doing her work when he arrived. When she came out, the crowd round the door, the majority of whom were hostile, asked her questions about his behaviour. Her answer was: "I don't know what he's done to deserve to be there, but I can tell you that he is a good man and that no one like him has ever been in the cell before. It would do anyone good to be near him and the way he talks and what he says would melt the hardest heart."

He was refused a minister of his own religion, but the Sheriff sent three Anglican clergymen into his cell to endeavour to convince him of his wickedness. They tried to make him admit his blood-guiltiness in the matter of the King's execution and the justness of his sentence, as well as of "being loose in family duties and the observation of the Lord's Day." For the last, he called his servant who had been with him continually for eight years and said: "Ask him." The servant answered that nothing could be more false and that his master was "wholly devoted to religious exercises and very zealous in observing the Lord's day" and "a great comfort and consolation to his whole family."

Regarding the charge of blood-guiltiness, Harrison reiterated what he had maintained at the trial: "What I did, I did by the authority of Parliament, which was then the only lawful authority, for God owned it, by pleading their cause and fighting their battles for them; the 'Lord's people' (the Puritan soldiers) owned it, by rejoicing in it and praying for it; the generality of people in England, Scotland and Ireland owned it, by yielding obedience to it; foreign Princes owned it, by sending Ambassadors to it. It was the act of the Parliament not ours who were Parliament's servants." As for 'the justness of the thing that was done upon him by reason of his iniquity,' he answered: "I am filled with God's peace and I am sure that this has not been given me on account of my iniquity."

The clergymen left him, saying that they had come because the Sheriff had sent them, but they would like to return on their own account.

Next morning, the Sheriff called on him to say that he must die in half an hour. "But the sheriff left him to stay a little longer and, in the meantime he was longing for the sheriff's coming and his friends judged that he was in haste to be gone. He said, he was going about a great work for the Lord that day and he looked upon this as a clear answer of his prayers; for many a time, he said, have I begged of the Lord that if He had any hard thing, any reproachful work or contemptible service to be done, that I should be employed in it; and now, blessed be God Who accounteth me worthy to be put upon this service for my Lord Christ."

He parted from his wife as if he were going on an ordinary journey, and gave her his Bible. This was all he had to leave her. He committed her to the care of his friends with "As you say you love me, show that love by being tender to my dear wife."

When at last the Keeper of the prison came to summon him, 'he ran downstairs with a cheerful countenance,' but found the door locked. In the Hall, where he had to wait till he was overtaken and the door opened, a woman came up and grasped his hand and shouted: "Blessed be the great God of Hosts that hath enabled you and called you forth to bear your testimony; the God of all grace and peace be with you and keep you faithful to death that you may receive a crown of life."

An officer took her roughly by the shoulder and pushed her back with: "Away with this prating woman."

"Don't be hard on her," said Harrison. "She is only quoting Scripture."

Still the procession of death did not start. Harrison was next locked in a room with the ordinary prisoners of Newgate. He spent the time in preaching to them about the love and mercy of God, ending with the warning: "Your time in this world is short and uncertain. You are walking on the brink of eternity and may drop in any moment. Labour to come to Christ!" Then he put his hand in his pocket and distributed what money he had, keeping only that which, by custom, he would give to the executioner.

The authorities had determined to do what they could to tire him out and break his nerve, so he was next taken up to the roof of Newgate and forced to go out on the leads from where he could see the city at his feet and the dense, jeering crowds through which he would have to pass to execution. His only comment was: "The earth is the Lord's and the fulness thereof; and there is nothing hid from His eyes."

At last he was hustled downstairs again to the waiting sledge. He helped them tie the rope on him, and said to the watching crowd: "According to the light God hath given me, I have served Him and my country, not wittingly or willingly wronging any."

"Then," says a contemporary account, "he was carried away in the sledge, having a sweet, smiling countenance, with his eyes and hands lifted up to heaven, his countenance never changing in all the way as he went to the place of execution, but was mighty cheerful, to the astonishment of many. As he was going to suffer, one in derision called to him and said: 'Where is now your Good Old Cause?' He, with a cheerful smile, clapped his hand on his breast and said: 'Here it is, and I am going to seal it with my blood.'"

The gallows had been set up by the stump of Charing Cross and he was made to stand looking towards the Banqueting House. He went up the ladder 'with an undaunted countenance' and in his short speech to the people reiterated: "Though I am wrongfully charged with murder and bloodshed, yet I must tell you that I have kept a good conscience towards God and towards man. I do declare, as one now almost before God's judgment, that I would not be guilty willingly or wittingly of the blood of the meanest son of England, no, not for ten thousand worlds, much less of the blood of such as I am charged with."

His hands and his legs started to shake and the people became loud in derision. He explained: "Gentlemen, by reason of your scoffing, I judge that you think I am afraid to die, because of the shaking I have in my hands and knees. But it is by reason of much blood I have lost in the wars and many wounds which has caused this weakness; I have had it for twelve years. And I have this morning, before I came here, been so hurried up and down stairs (for what purpose I do not know) that my spirits are almost spent."

In spite of the ague, he continued speaking, in the same strain as he had spoken to the prisoners in Newgate, and ended: "And now I desire to commit myself into the hands of our Lord and Saviour Jesus Christ, who delivered himself for the chief of sinners: He that came into the world, was made flesh and was crucified; that hath loved me and washed me from my sins with His own blood, and is risen again, sitting at the right hand of God, making intercession for me. I have served a good Lord and Master, who hath helped me from my beginning to this day, and hath carried me through many difficulties, trials, straits and temptations and hath always been a very present help in time of trouble. He hath covered my head many times in the day of battle. By my God

I have leaped over a wall: by my God I have run through a troop and by my God I will go through this death and He will make it easy to me. Now, into Thy hands, O Lord Jesus, I commit my spirit."

He was turned off the ladder and his body cut down immediately so that he should be fully conscious while he was castrated and disembowelled. In the extremity of this agony, he reached out with one of his hands and 'gave the executioner a box on the ear.' One reporter commented: "This sentence was so barbarously executed that he saw his bowels thrown into the fire" and Mr. Pepys recorded that the blood-lust of the crowd was such that "when his head and heart were shown to the people, there were great shouts of joy." His limbs were disjointed and carried back to Newgate on the same hurdle that had brought him to Charing Cross, and subsequently exhibited over London Bridge and at other places.

There was, in Harrison's trial and death, "no attempt to escape,[1] no paltering with his conscience as to the work he had done or the motives that had led him on, no faltering in his resignation to his fate, in his reliance on the support of the Most High, or in his courage and fortitude under the torture of his prison and the inhuman barbarity of his death. He had not, like the King, the solace of knowing that multitudes of his fellow-countrymen mourned with him and for him and would at a convenient moment, rise again to restore his family and his name. He had not the companionship, in his last days, of his own minister of religion and the society of dear and loyal friends. Harrison's party were then beaten and discredited; many of his friends were in gaol, others were awaiting the last sentence of the law, and he had himself spent months in prison. He was not led as a soldier to his death with the pomp of arms and the clanging of accoutrements, but, his body emaciated by fasting and his

[1] He had proudly refused to flee to the Continent at the Restoration.

limbs bruised and wounded by manacles of iron, he was drawn to the scaffold with ignominy and shame. And yet, taking these two as Christian against Christian, and as man against man, can it be said that, in the supreme hour of their fate, courage, dignity and fortitude were more fully exemplified in the instance of the King than in that of the Independent?"

That question, posed by Inderwick seventy years ago, has been studiously ignored; yet it is only by attempting to answer it that the day they killed the King can be seen steadily and whole. For posterity, the gibbet at Charing Cross towers above the scaffold at Whitehall and, it may be, in the opinion of some dwarfs it a little.